SYNCOPATION IN 3/4
RHYTHM READING TEXT IN WALTZ TIME

Skip Note Publishing

8738 N. Peninsular Ave. Portland, OR 97217 USA (503)380-9259

Visit **Cruise Ship Drummer!** at www.cruiseshipdrummer.com

Contents

Introduction..3

How to use this book...3

Quarter notes...**6**

   20 bar exercise...8

   32 bar exercise...9

Quarter notes – linear...**10**

   20 bar exercise...12

   32 bar exercise...13

8th notes...**14**

   20 bar exercise...16

   32 bar exercise...17

8th rests..**18**

   20 bar exercise...20

   32 bar exercise...21

8th notes – ties..**22**

   20 bar exercise...24

   32 bar exercise...25

Syncopation...**26**

   Syncopation - two measures...29

Syncopation Exercise 1..**30**

Syncopation Exercise 2..**31**

Syncopation Exercise 3..**32**

Syncopation Exercise 4..**33**

Syncopation Exercise 5..**34**

Syncopation Exercise 6..**35**

Syncopation Exercise 7..**36**

Syncopation Exercise 8..**37**

Bibliography...**38**

About the author...**38**

Introduction

This volume is part 1 of an unofficial companion to a major book in the literature of drumming, **Progressive Steps To Syncopation** by Ted Reed. The general concept and presentation is similar to Reed, but the exercises are newly composed in 3/4 time. I have added a few subjects not present in the original book, and shortened or eliminated some subjects. This book covers jazz-style rhythms in quarter notes and 8th notes; additional volumes to be released in 2019 and after will deal with reading triplets and 16th notes in 3/4.

How to use this book

Like **Progressive Steps to Syncopation**, this book is written with a conventional "snare drum" line and "bass drum" line, but I encourage you to think of it differently. Think of the main rhythm part as a universal melody rhythm which you will interpret and orchestrate on the drums; you can usually ignore the stems-down part, or interpret it as beat marks to aid in interpreting the more difficult syncopated rhythms. One section where you should actually play both parts is the linear quarter note section; you can interpret the parts as snare drum and bass drum, or as any high and low sound, or as any two limbs.

The ways of applying the exercises to the drumset are endless, but here are some of the fundamental concepts involved. The following examples are all based on this practice rhythm:

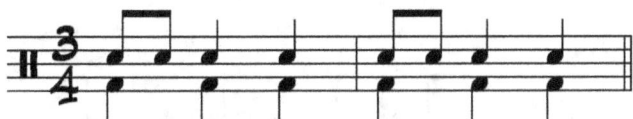

Play the melody rhythm along with an ostinato. For example, play the melody as a comping rhythm on the snare drum or bass drum while playing a jazz time feel (here a jazz waltz) with the cymbal, hihats, and bass drum:

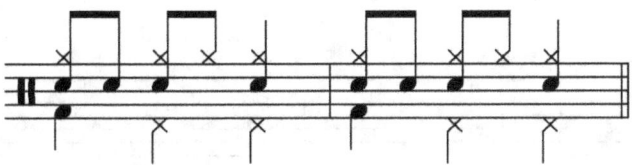

Swinging the rhythm. When practicing music with a swing feel, play the written 8th notes as parts of a triplet:

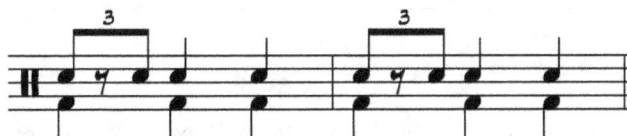

Revoicing the melody between two or more drums/sounds. For example, alternating between two sounds:

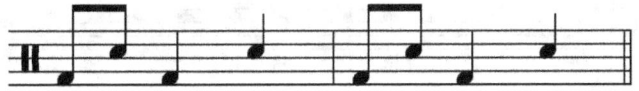

Often this is done with short notes (untied 8th notes) on the snare drum, and long notes (everything else: tied 8ths, quarter notes, dotted quarter notes) on the bass drum:

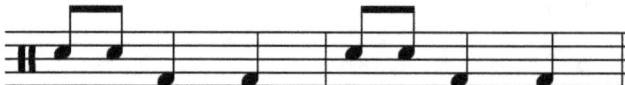

Filling in the rhythm. Filling in between the notes of the written rhythm, to make an unbroken rhythmic flow. The melody rhythm is still emphasized, often by accenting it, while "ghosting" the filler notes:

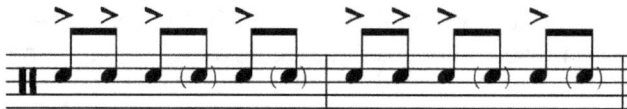

Or by orchestrating the melody/filler on the drums and/or cymbals. Here the melody is played on a cymbal and bass drum, and the filler notes are played quietly on the snare:

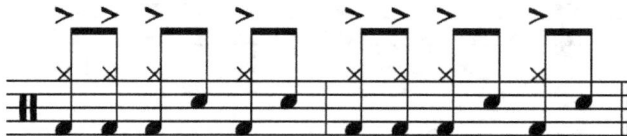

When playing a swing interpretation, you can fill out the rhythm with swing 8th notes, or 8th note triplets:

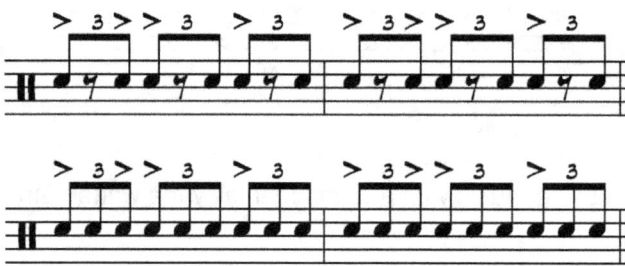

Many practice systems are based on varying the sticking of the melody rhythm + filler. For example, an alternating sticking:

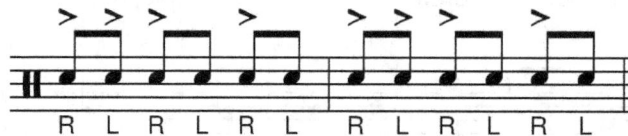

Or with the right-hand playing the melody rhythm and the left hand filling in:

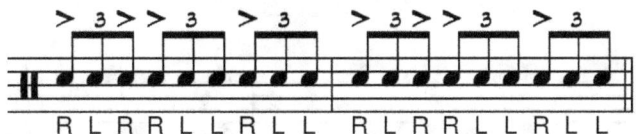

Or various rudimental stickings— for example, paradiddles:

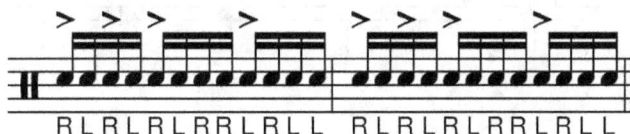

The rhythm can also be played on the snare drum and bass drum, with a cymbal rhythm added, to make various rock/funk/R&B/pop time feels:

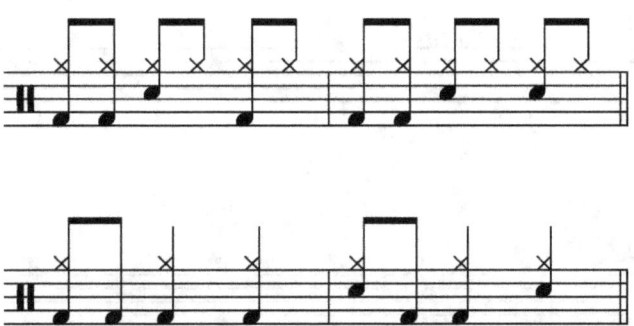

Visit **cruiseshipdrummer.com** and see our future e-books on Amazon for detailed practice methods.

Todd Bishop is also available for private lessons in these methods worldwide via Skype.

Quarter notes

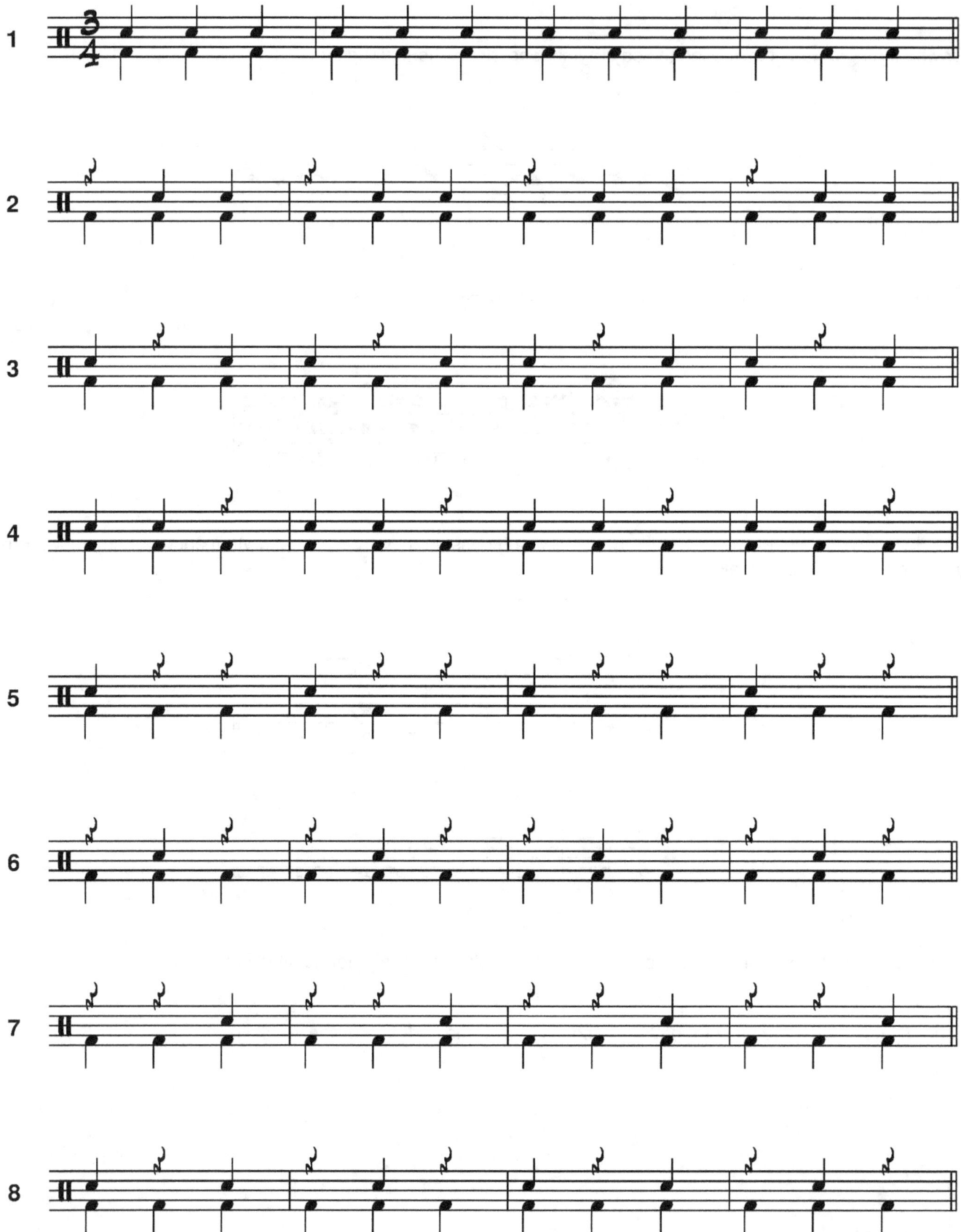

Quarter notes

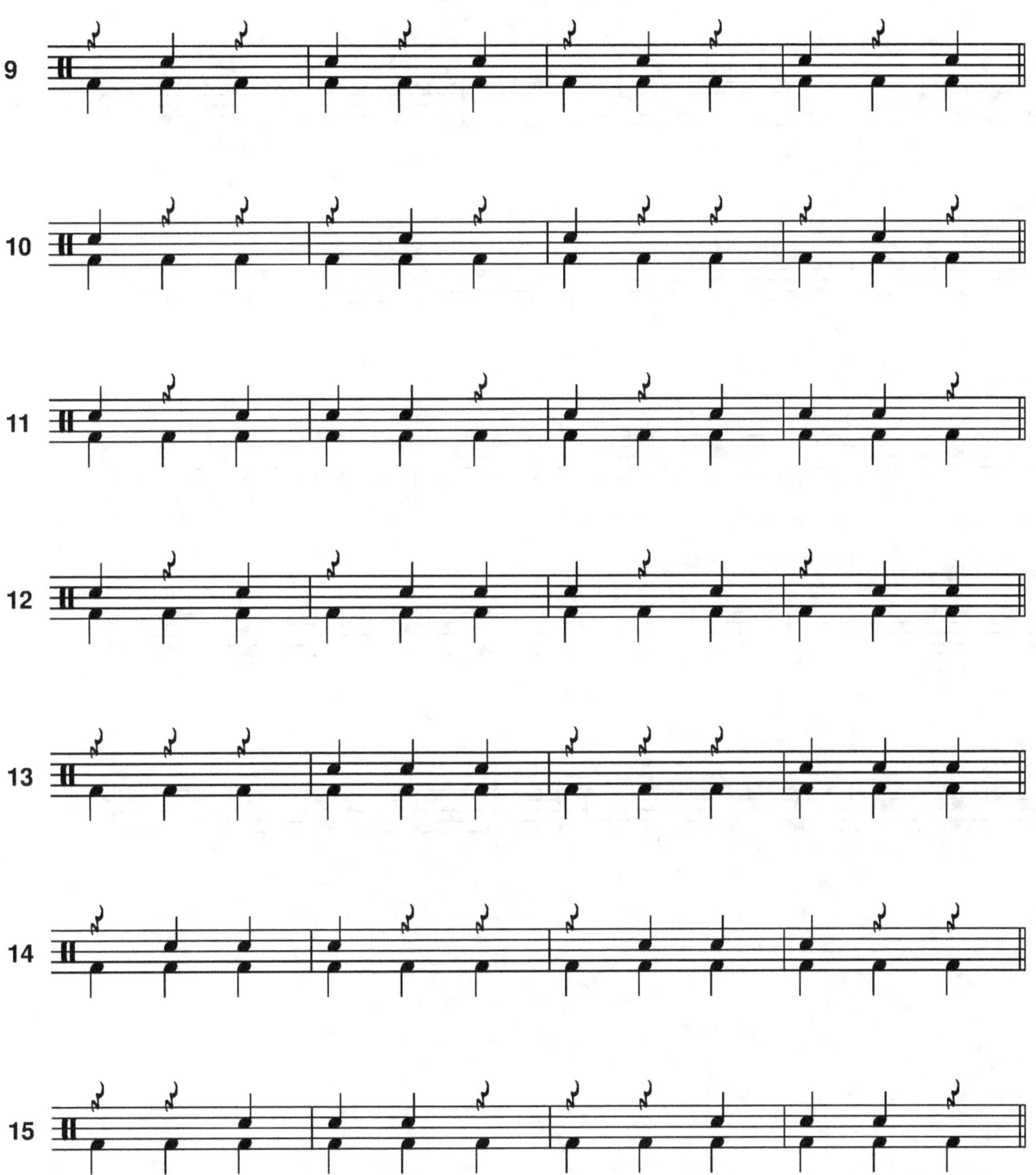

20 bar exercise

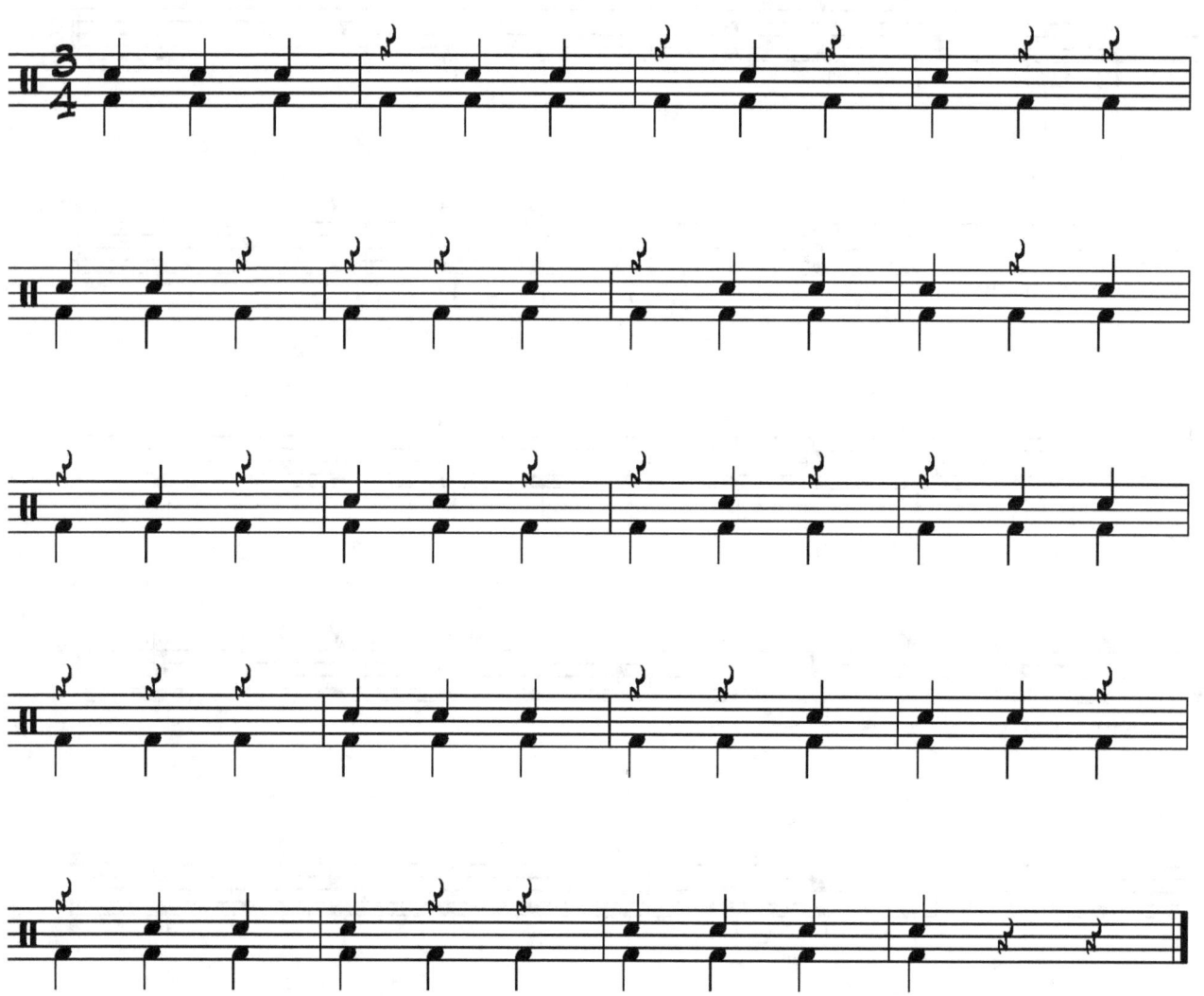

32 bar exercise

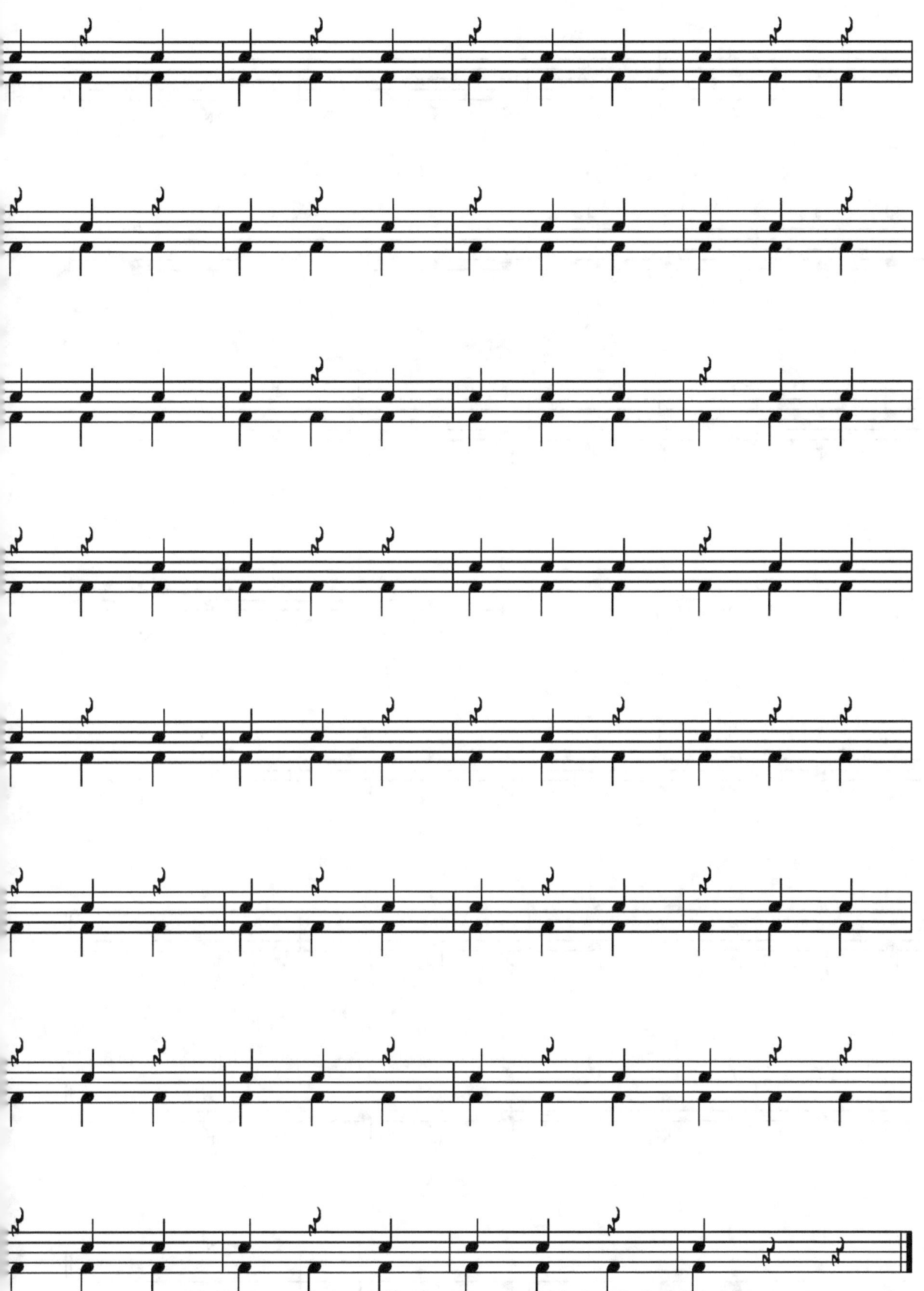

Quarter notes – linear

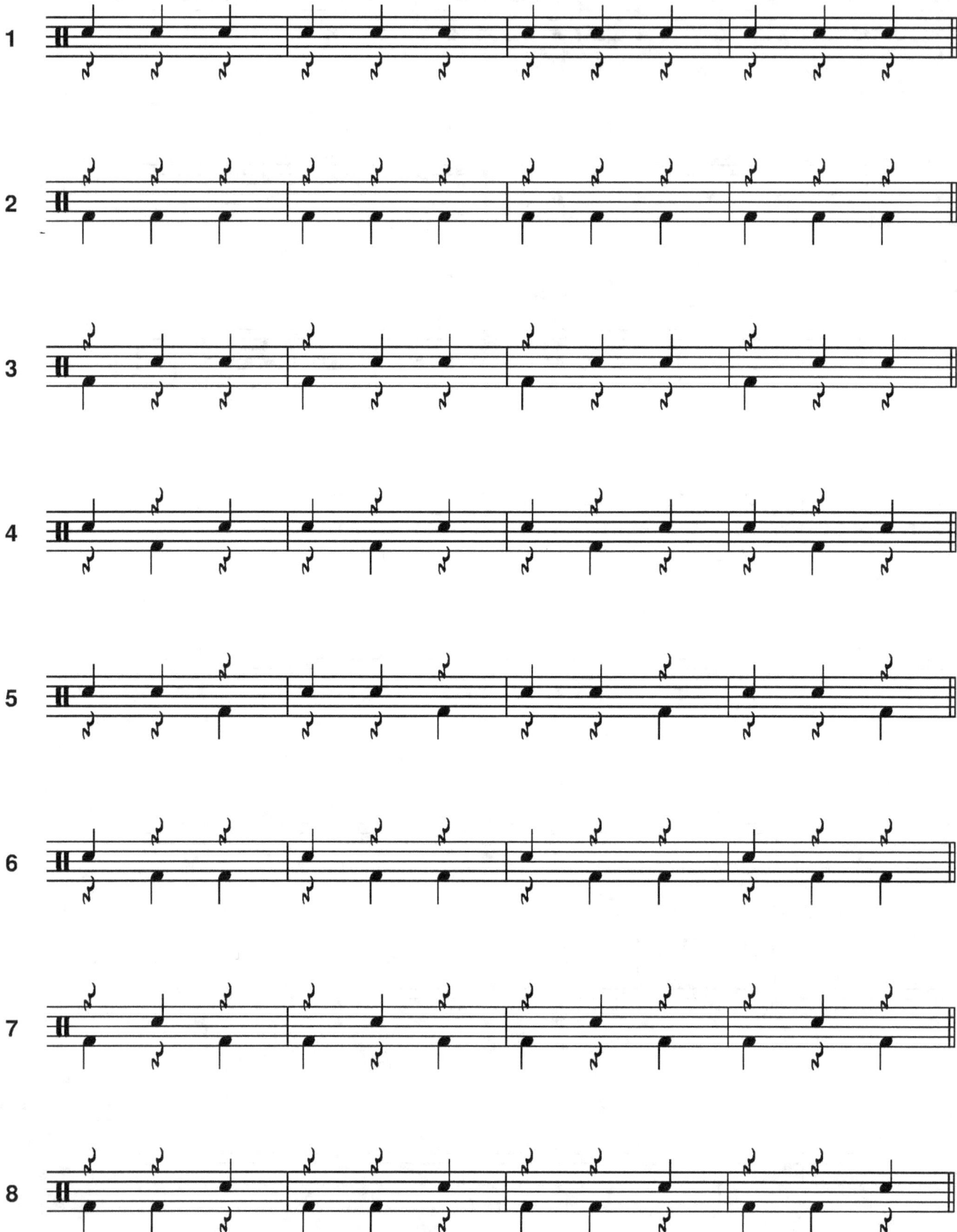

Quarter notes - linear

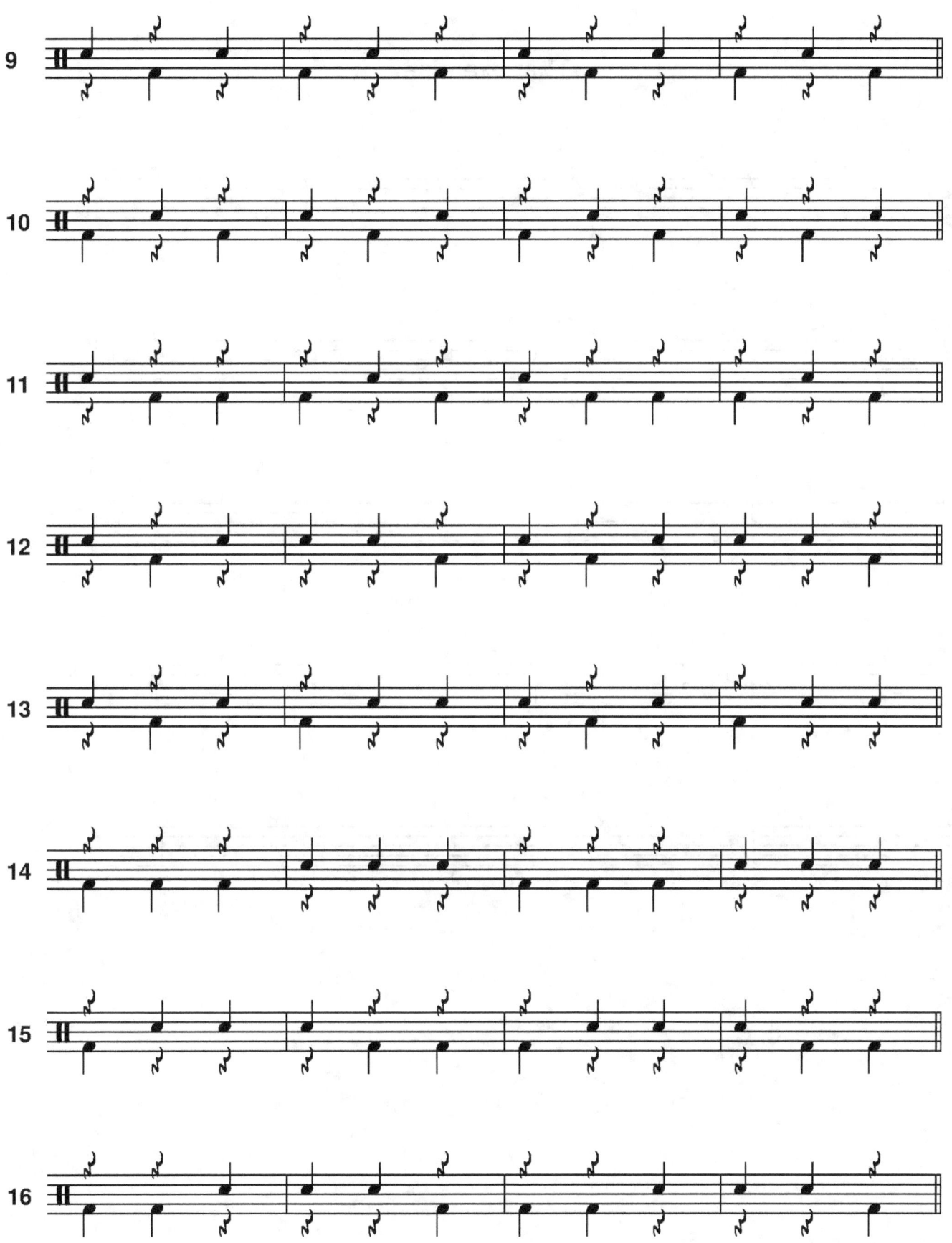

20 bar exercise

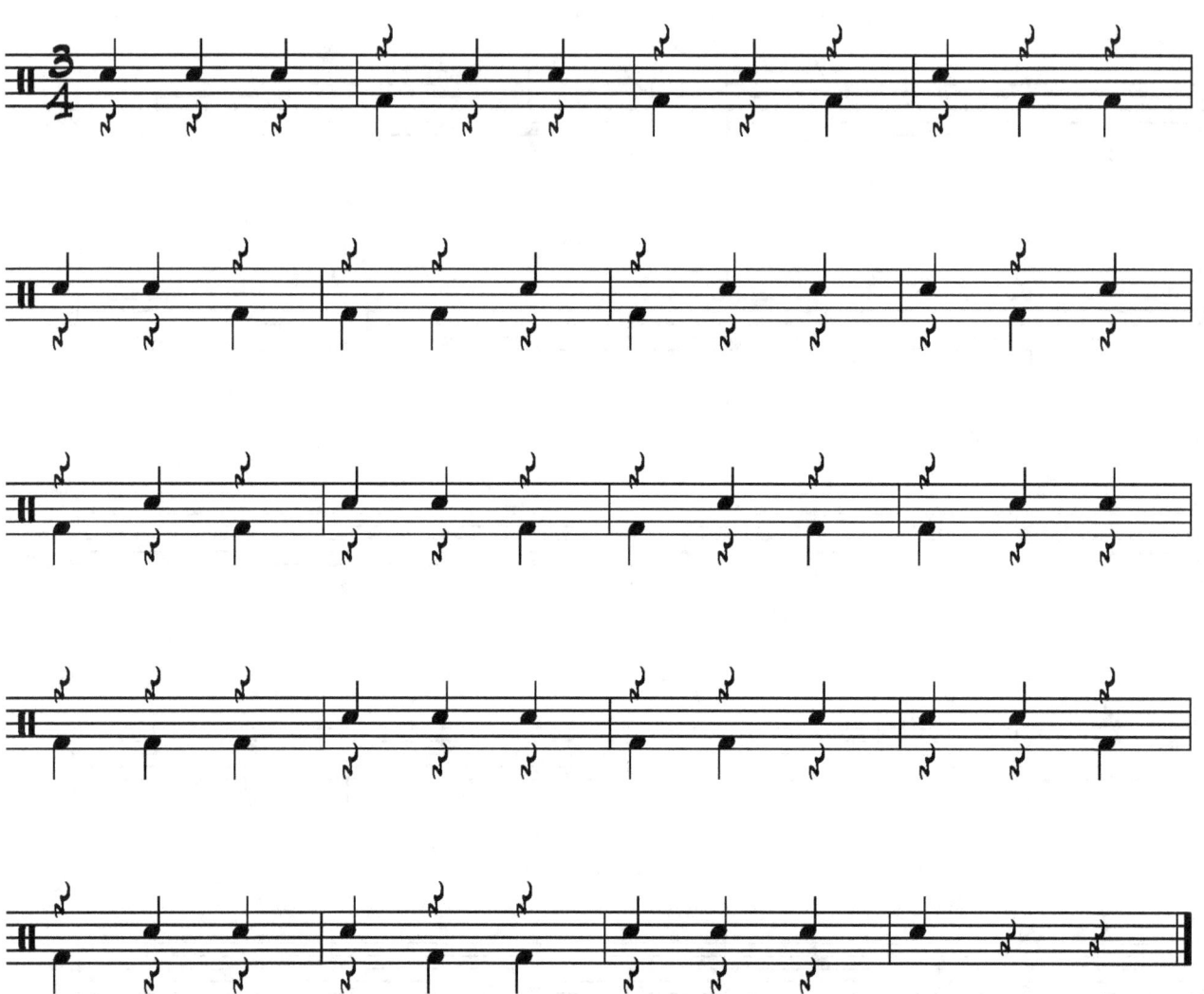

32 bar exercise

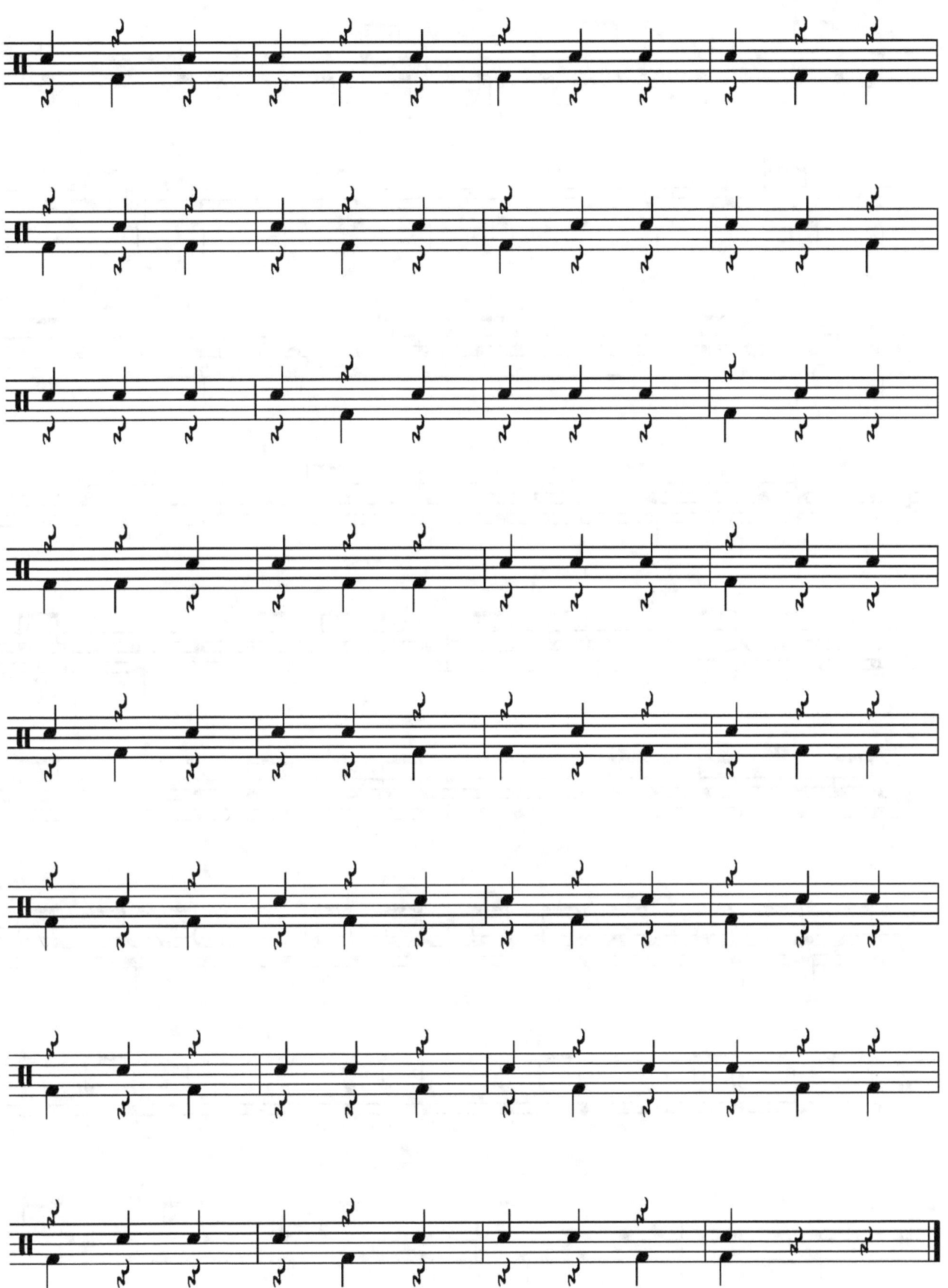

8th notes

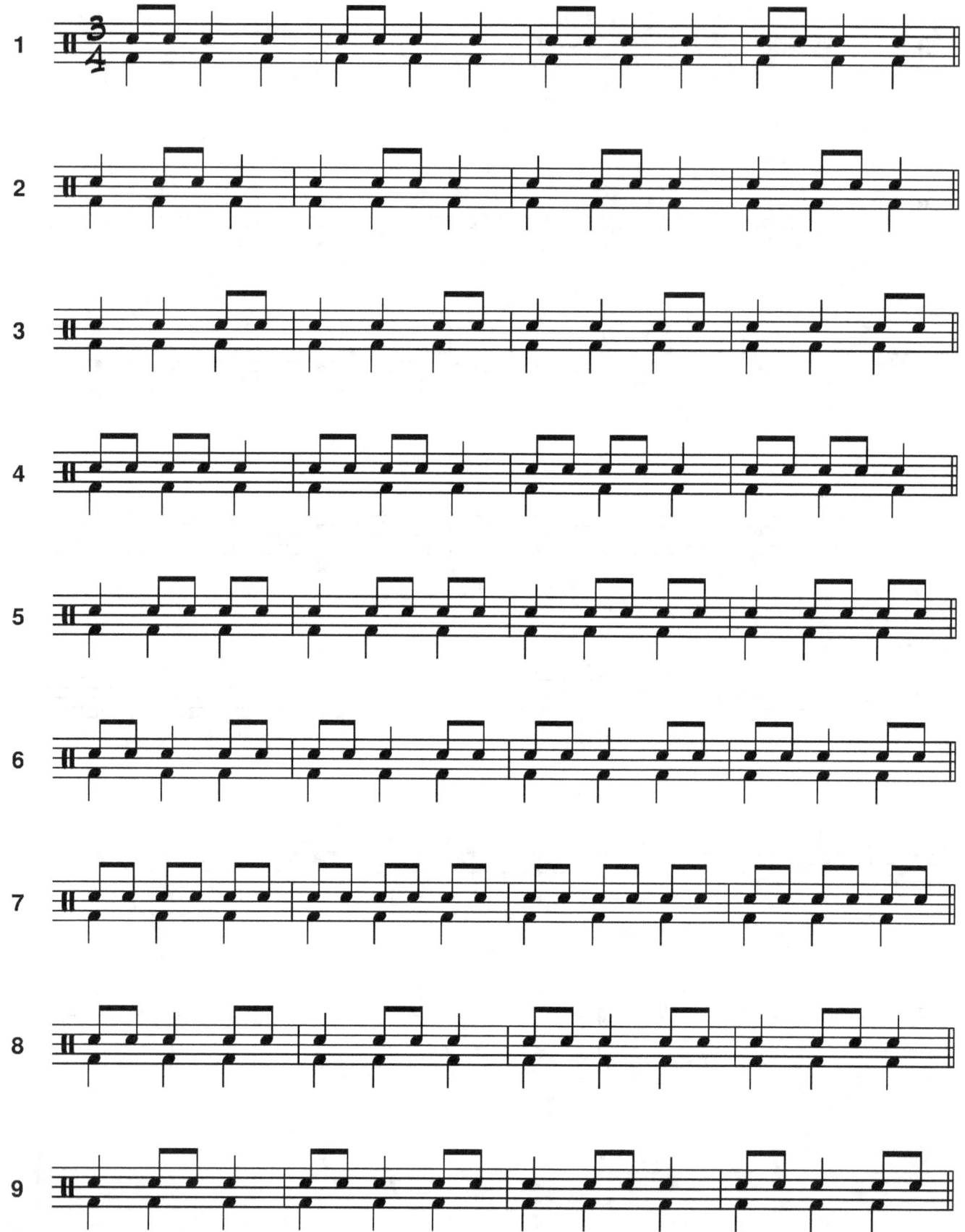

8th notes

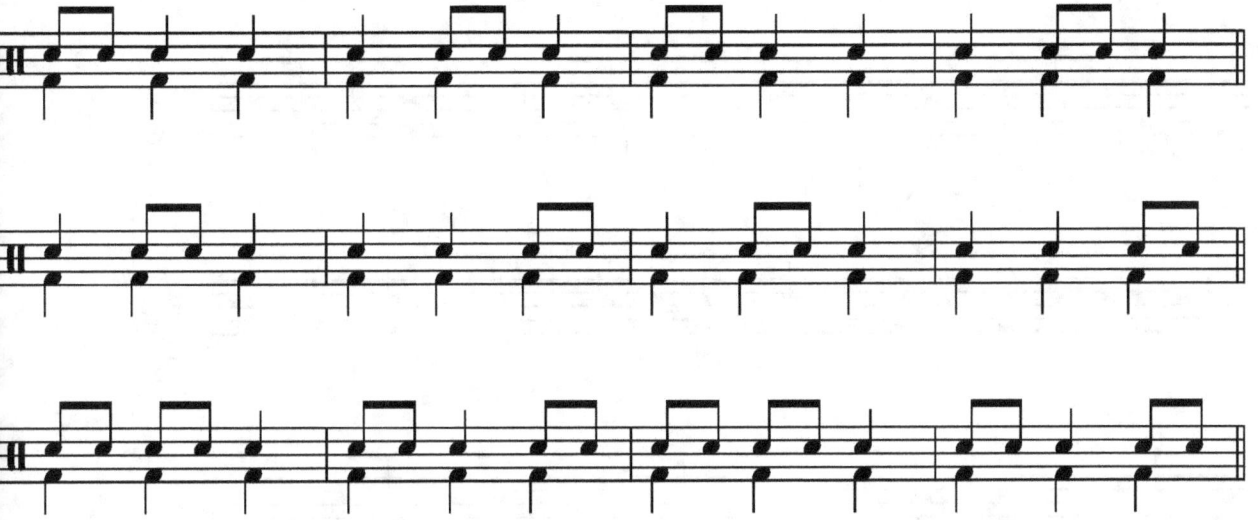

20 bar exercise

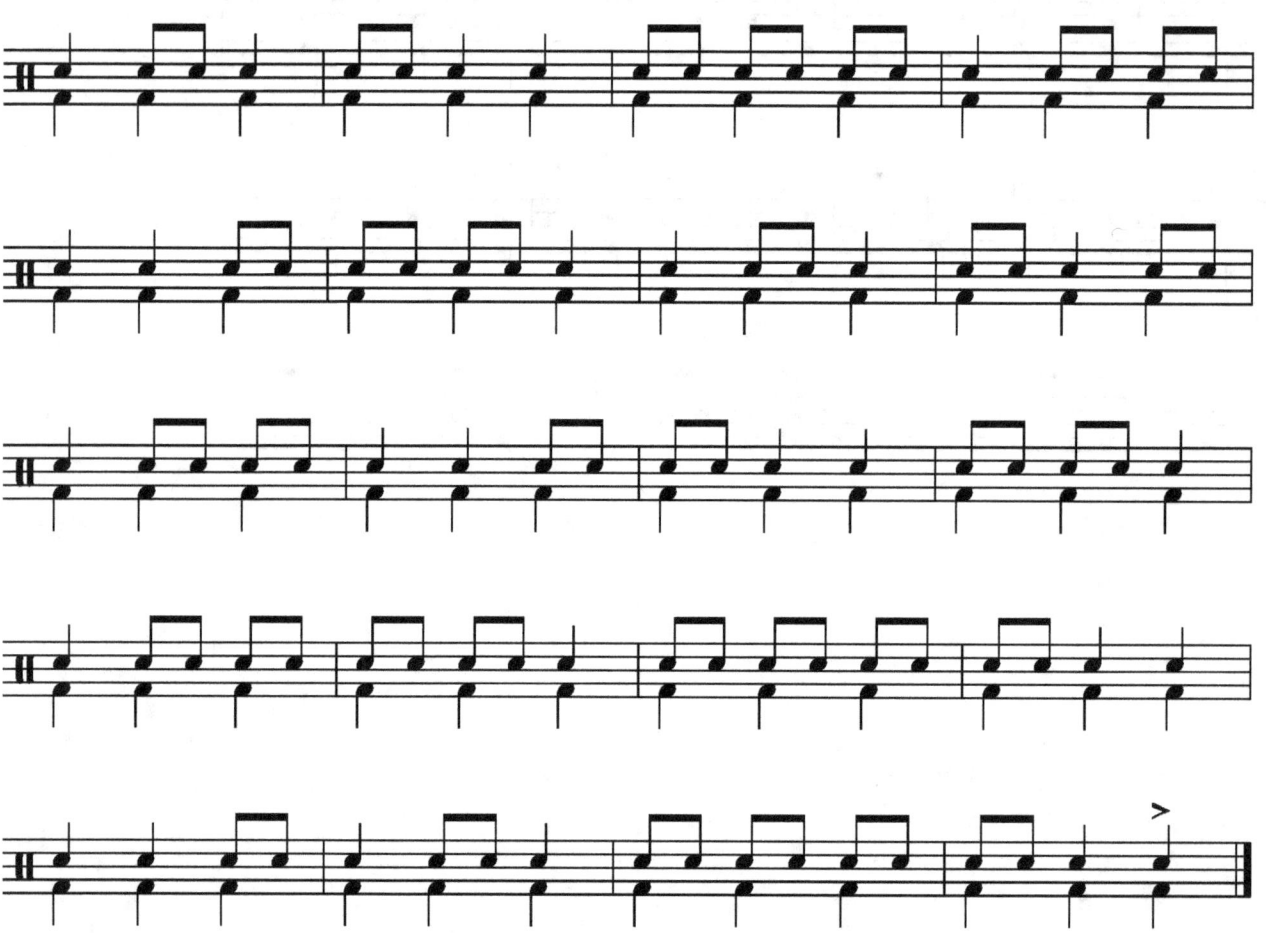

32 bar exercise

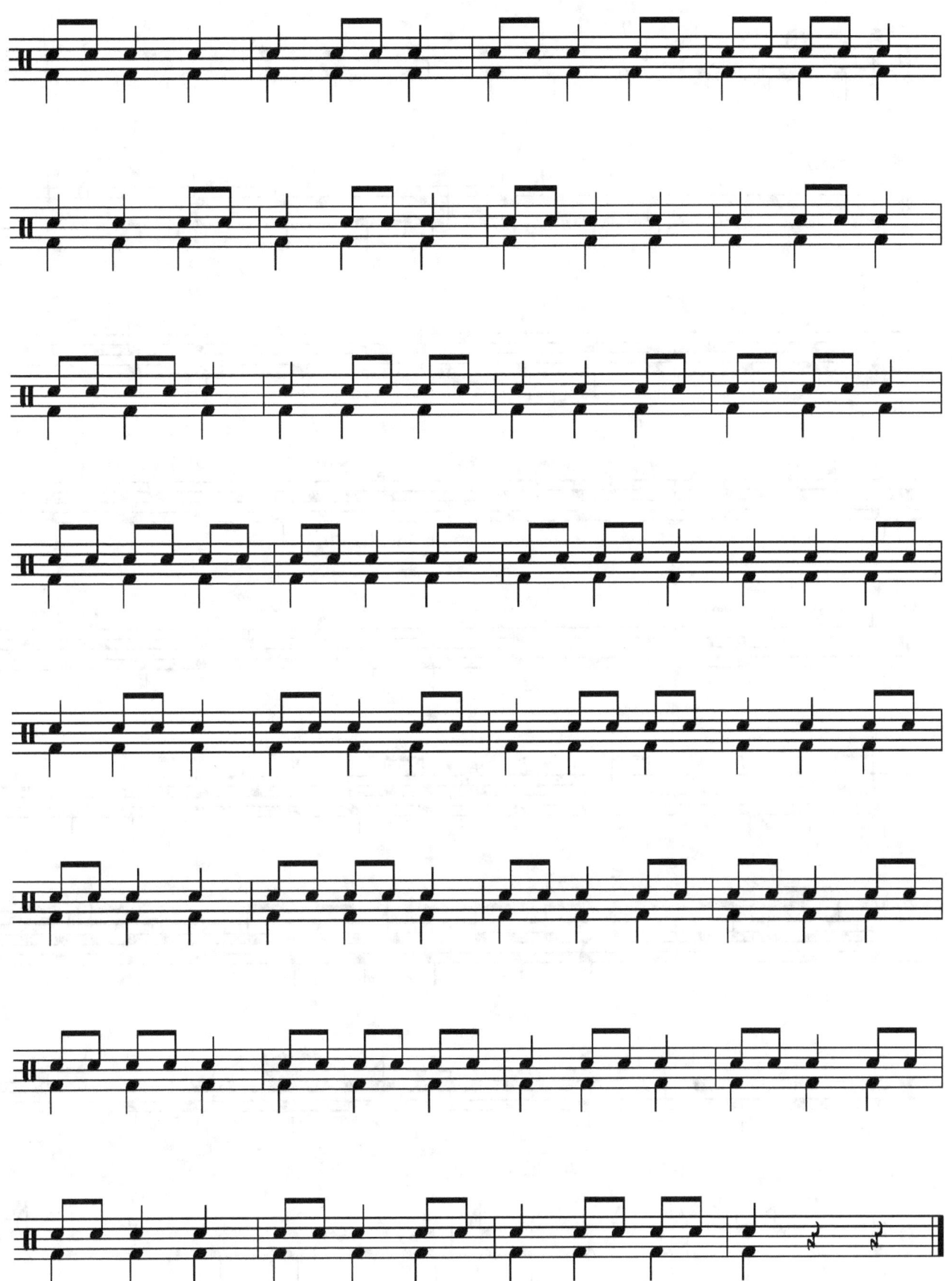

8th rests

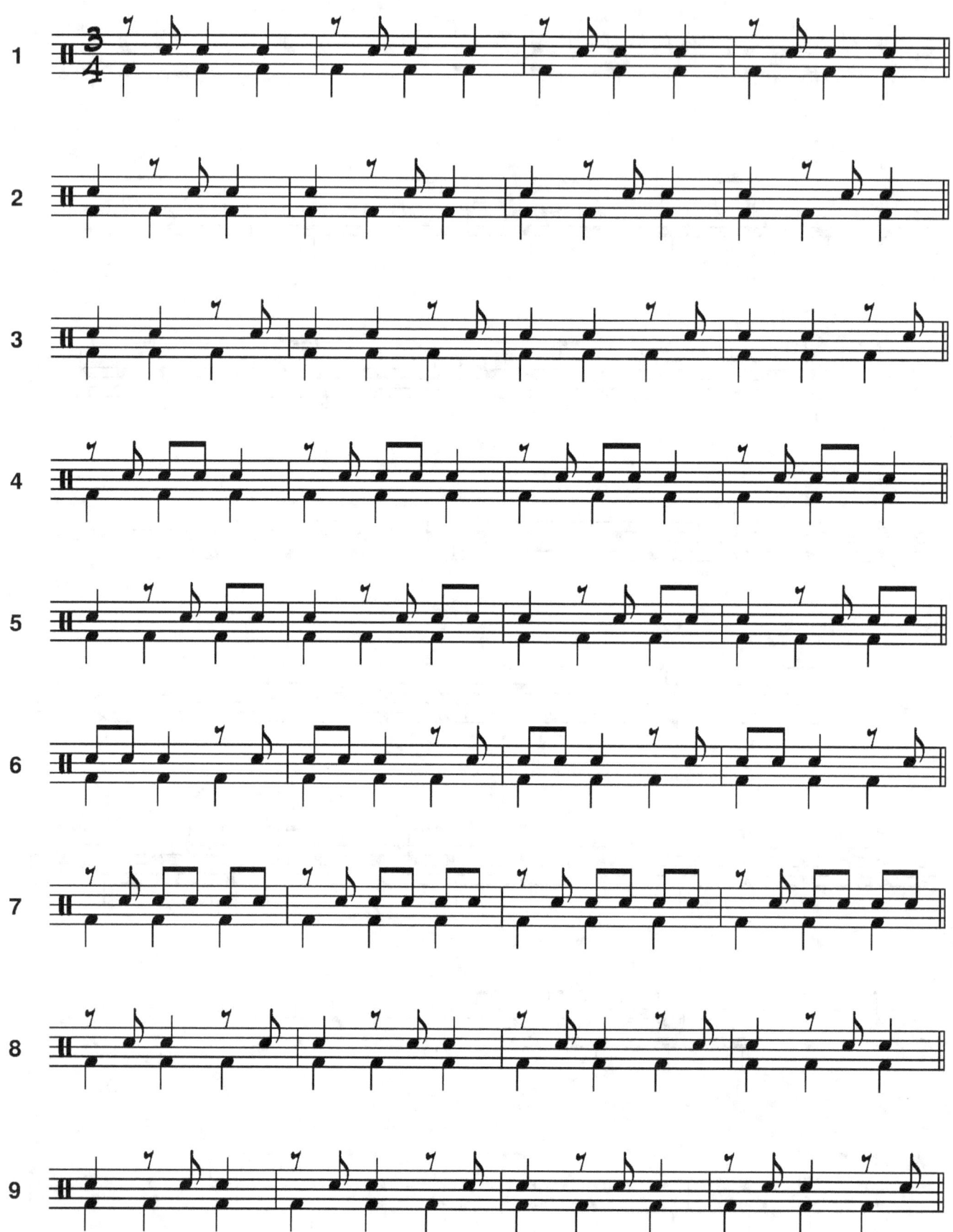

8ᵗʰ rests

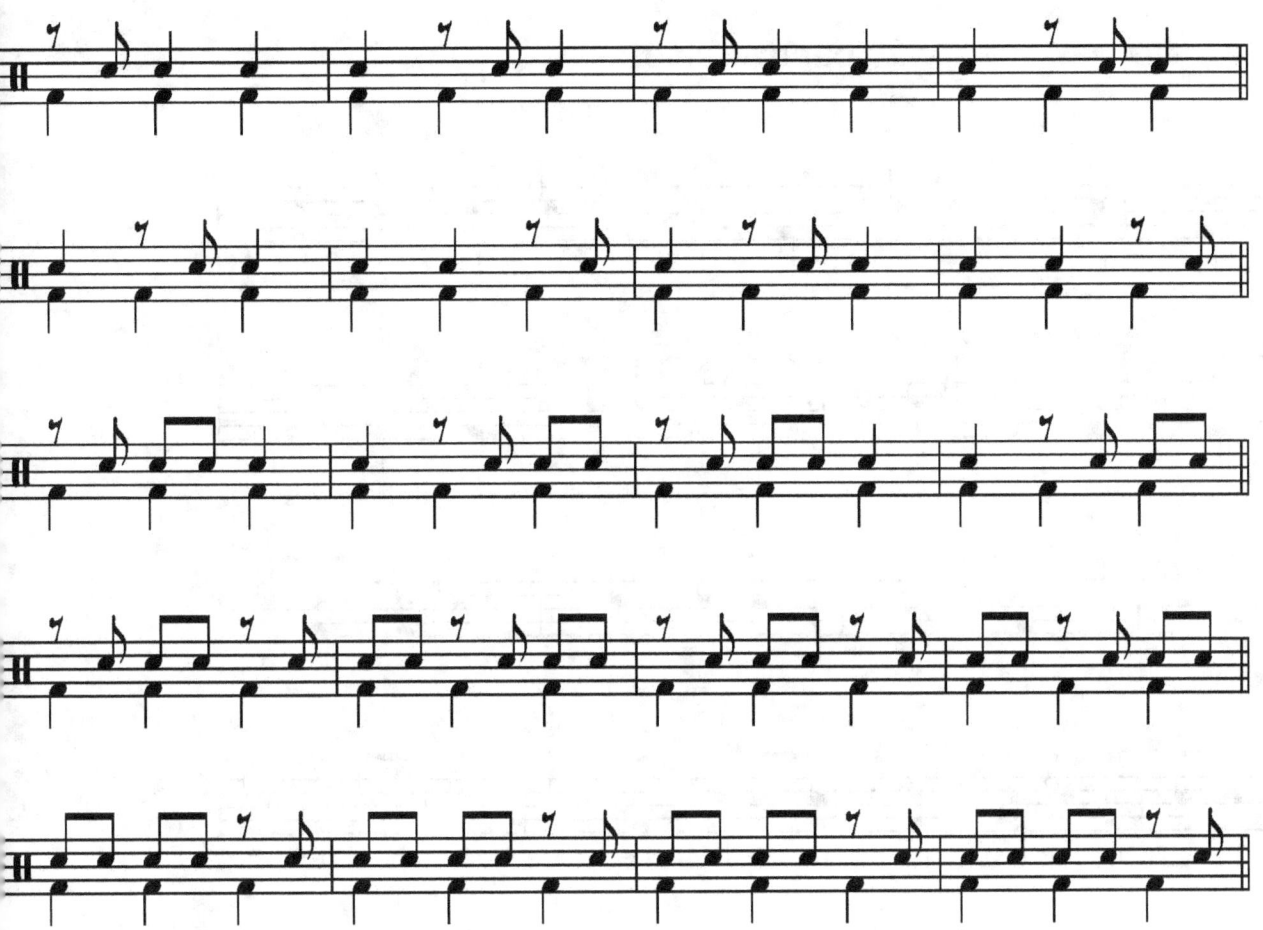

20 bar exercise

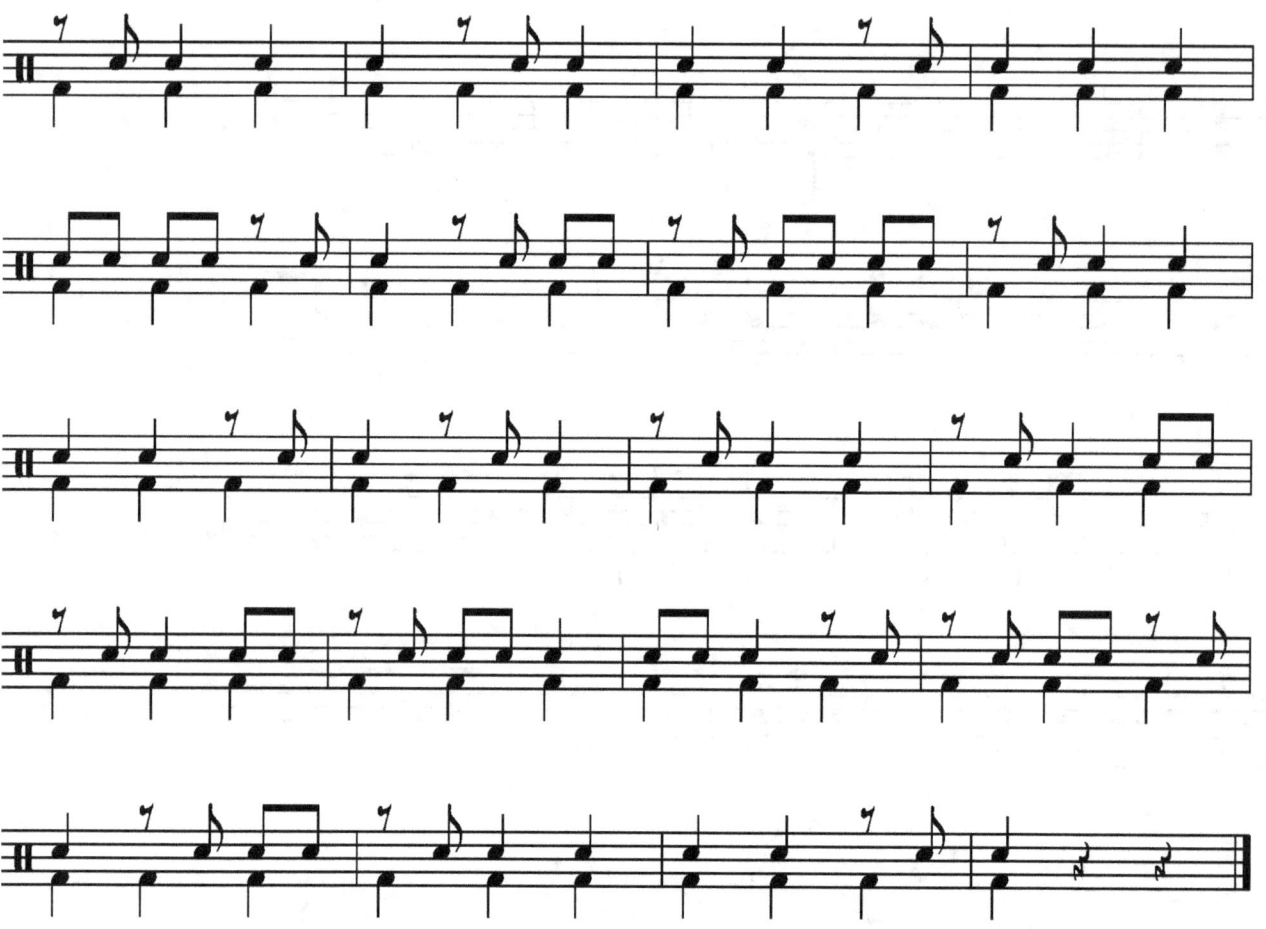

32 bar exercise

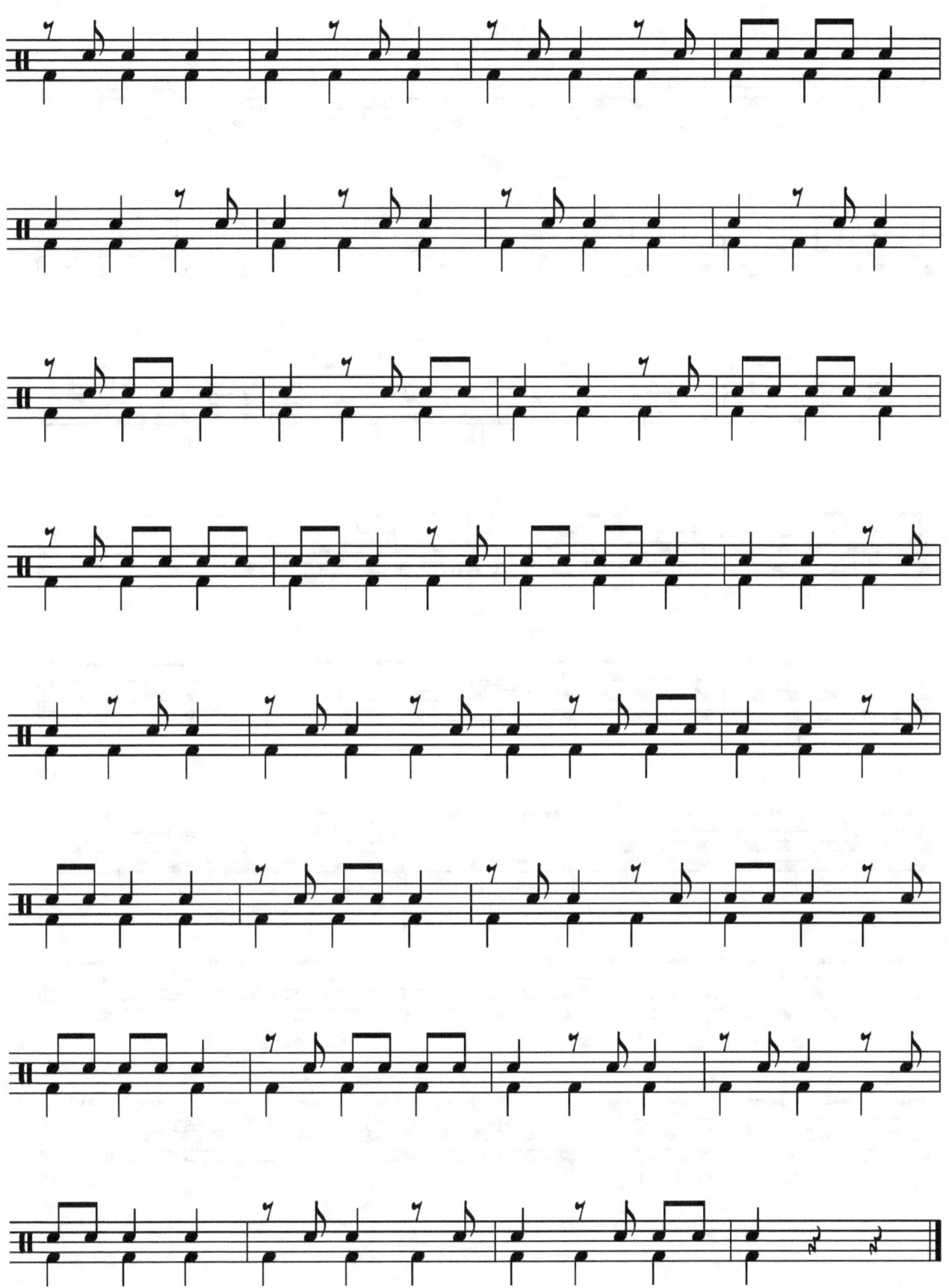

8th notes – ties

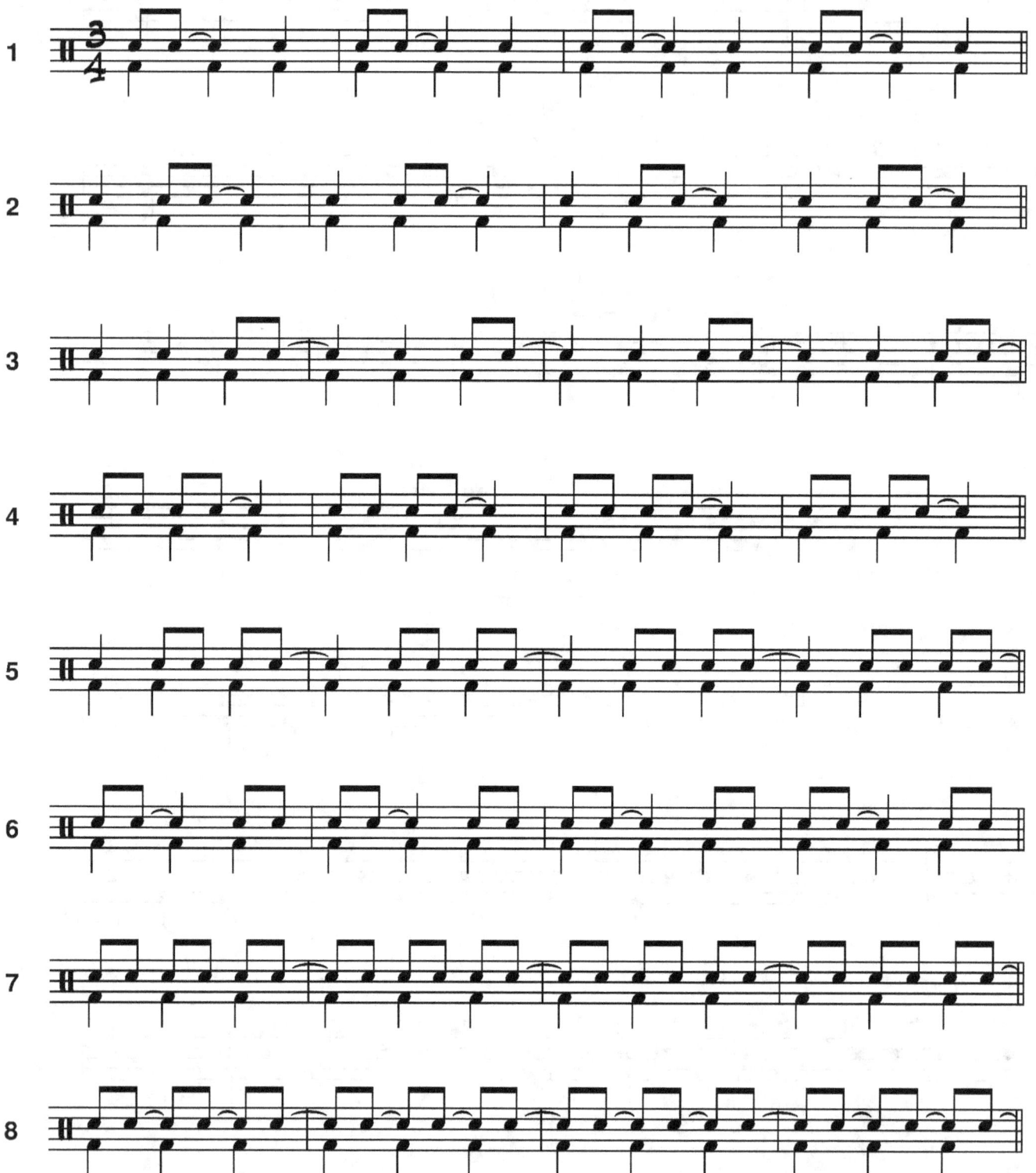

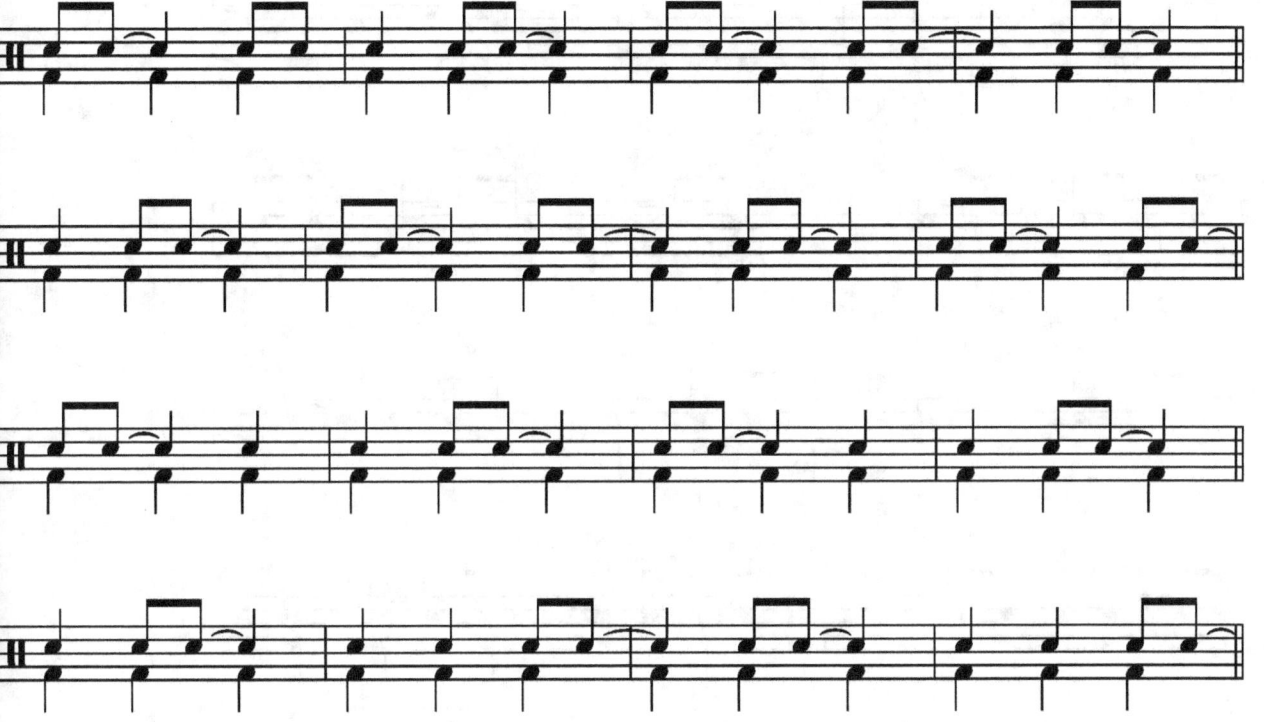

20 bar exercise

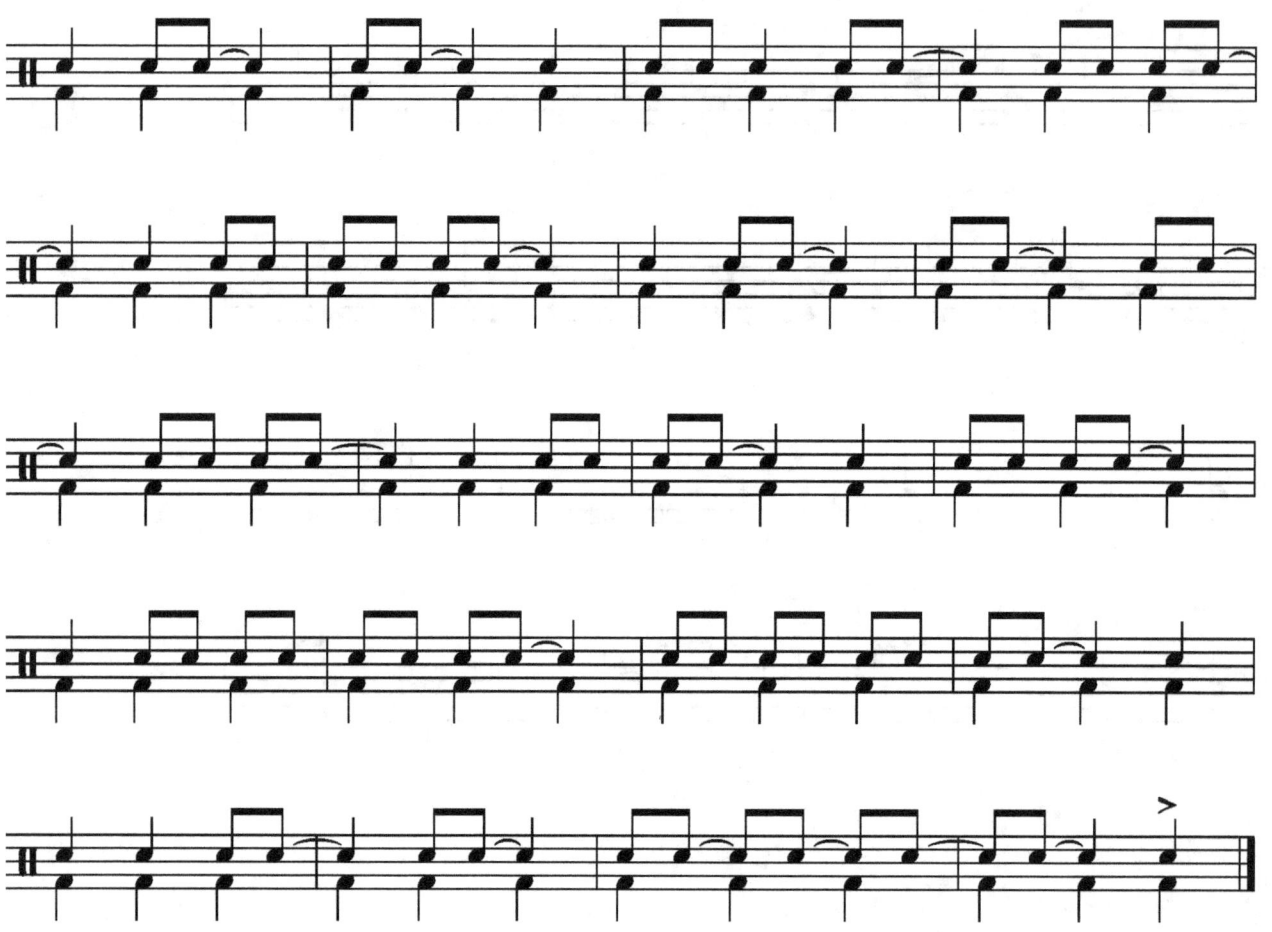

32 bar exercise

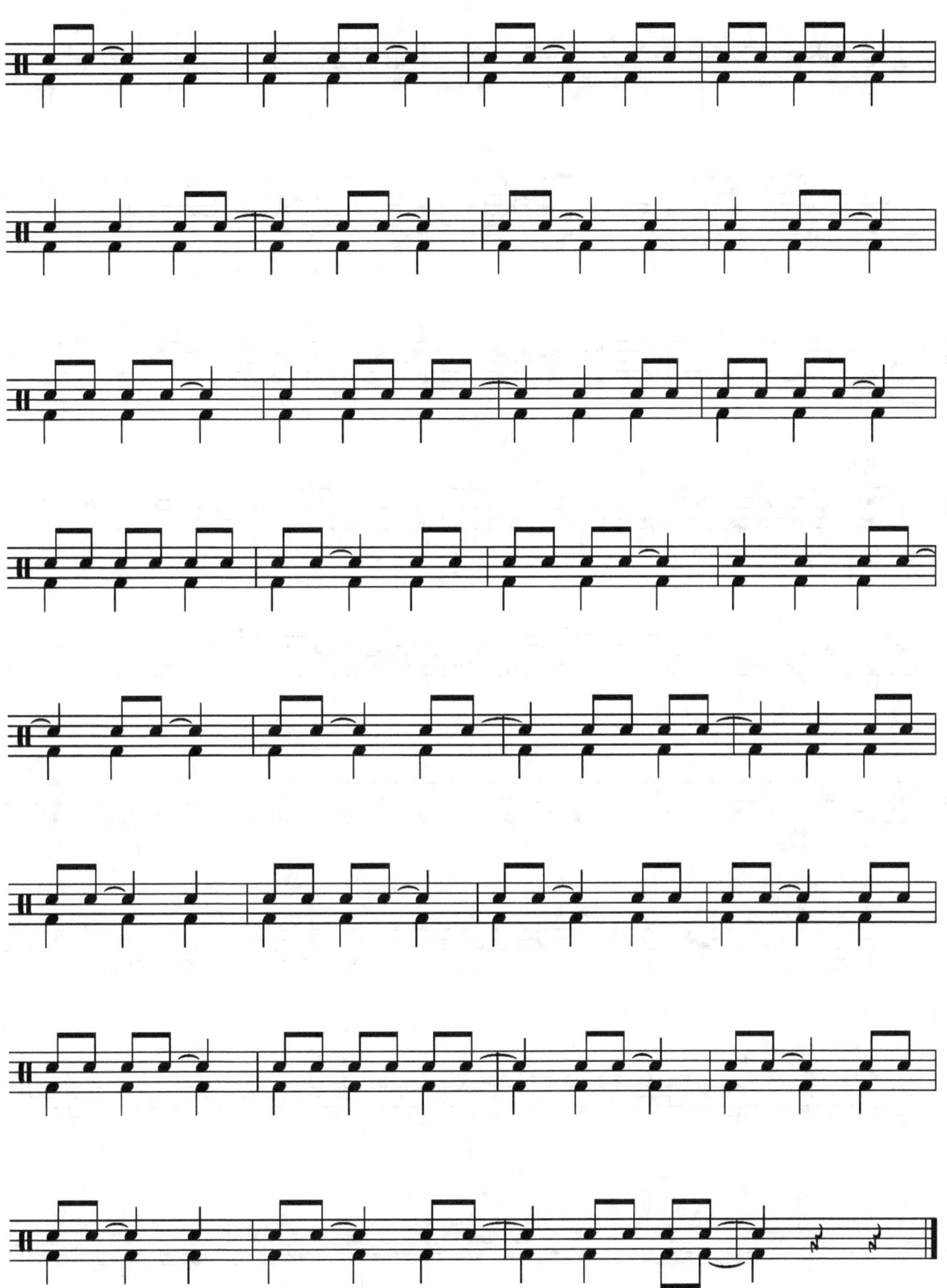

Syncopation

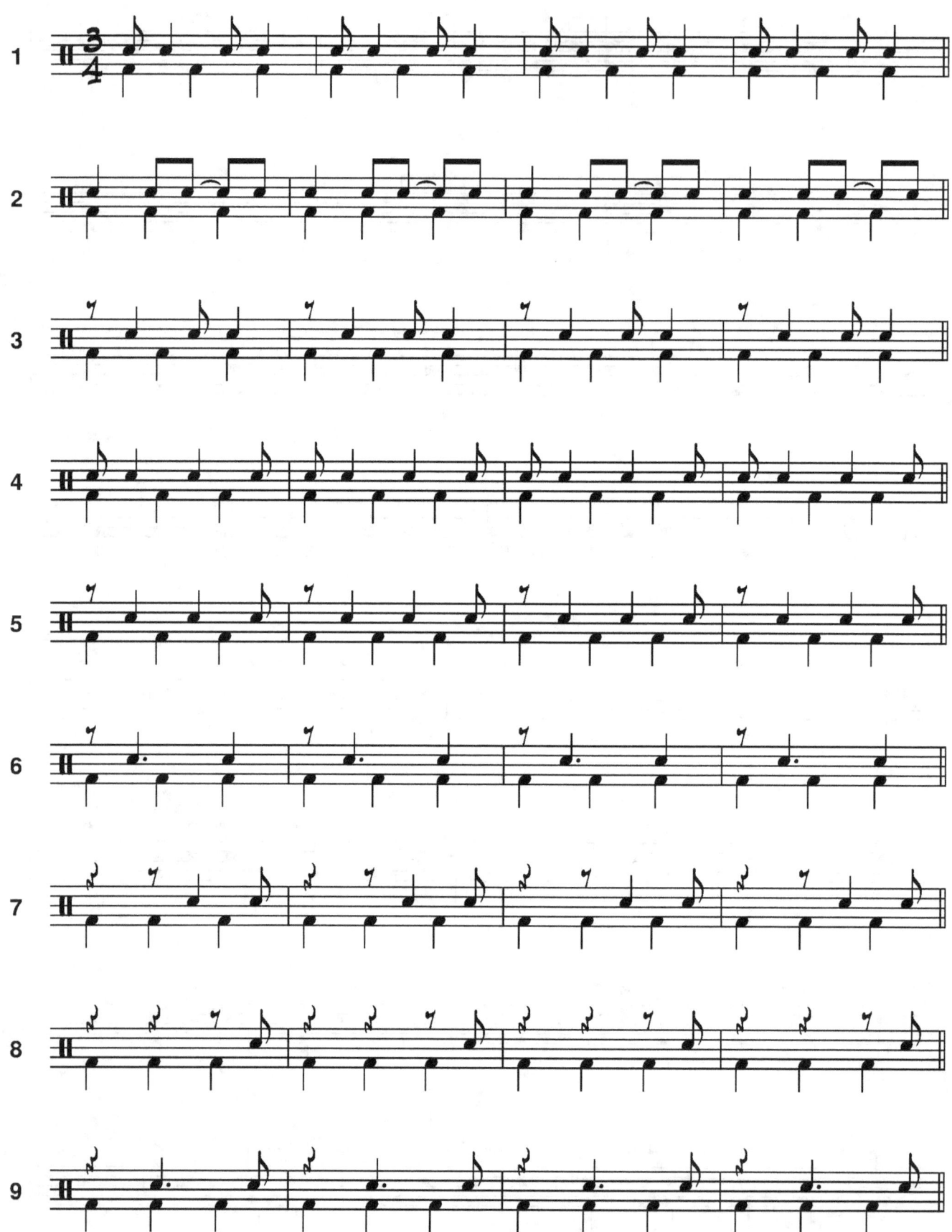

Syncopation

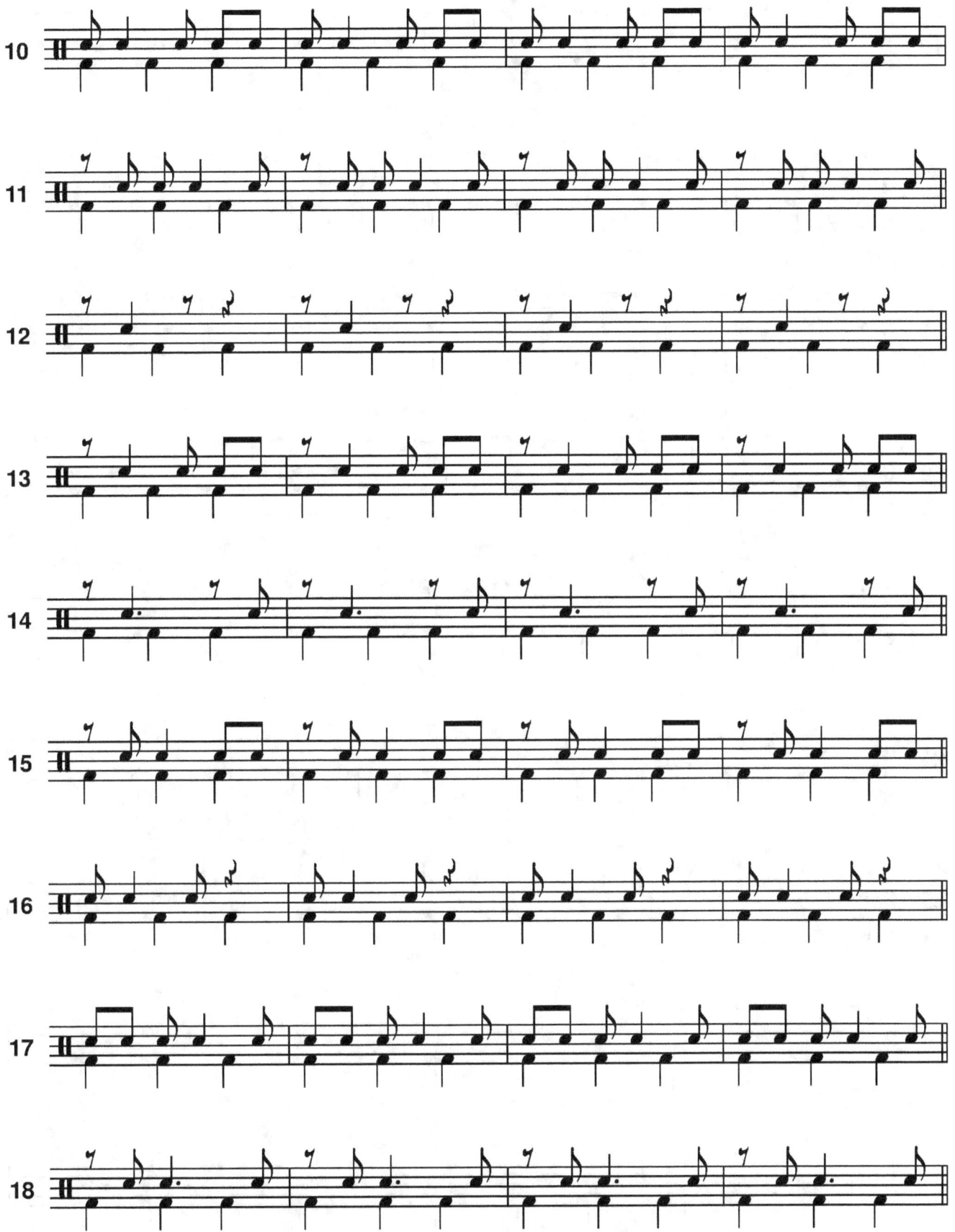

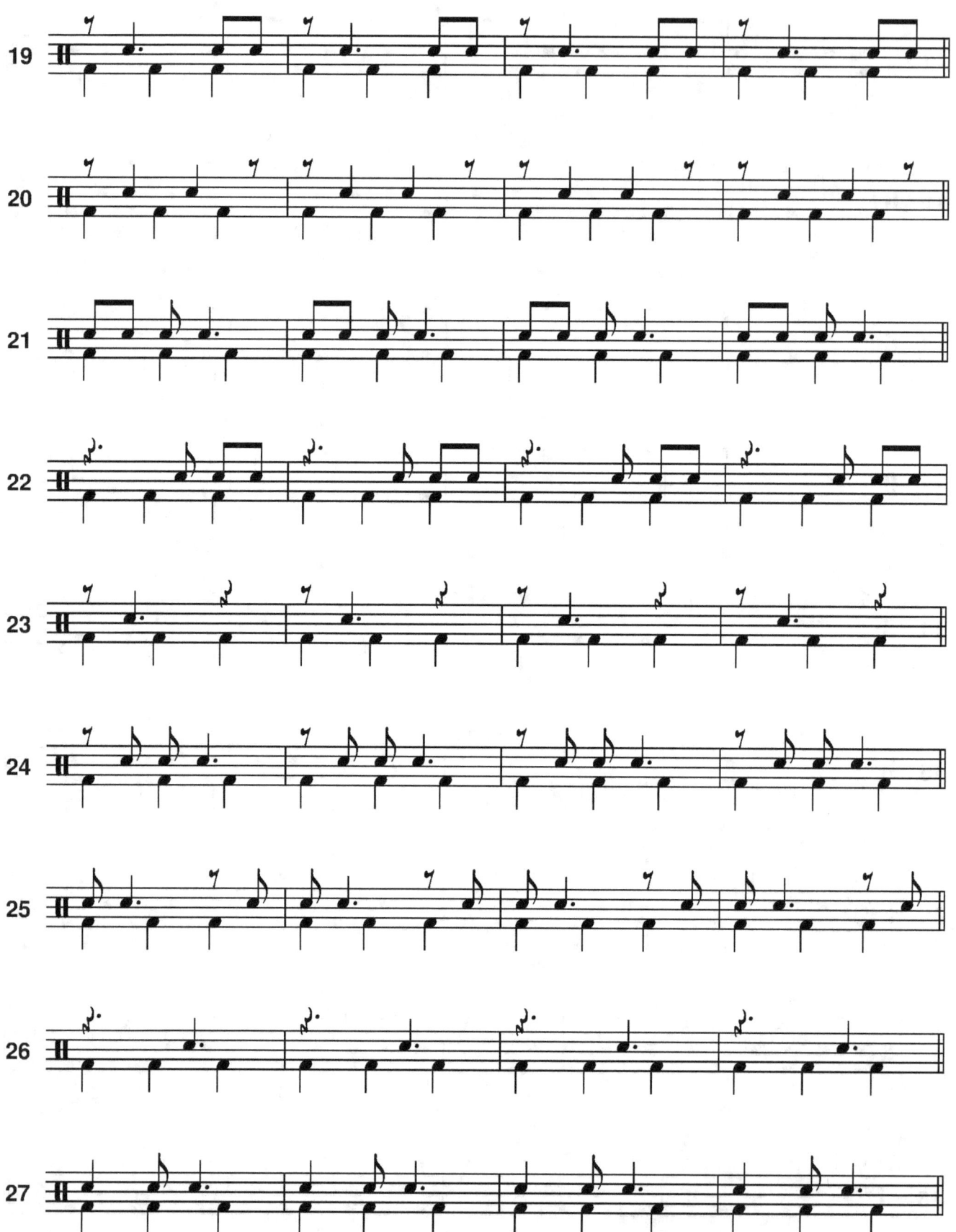

Syncopation - two measures

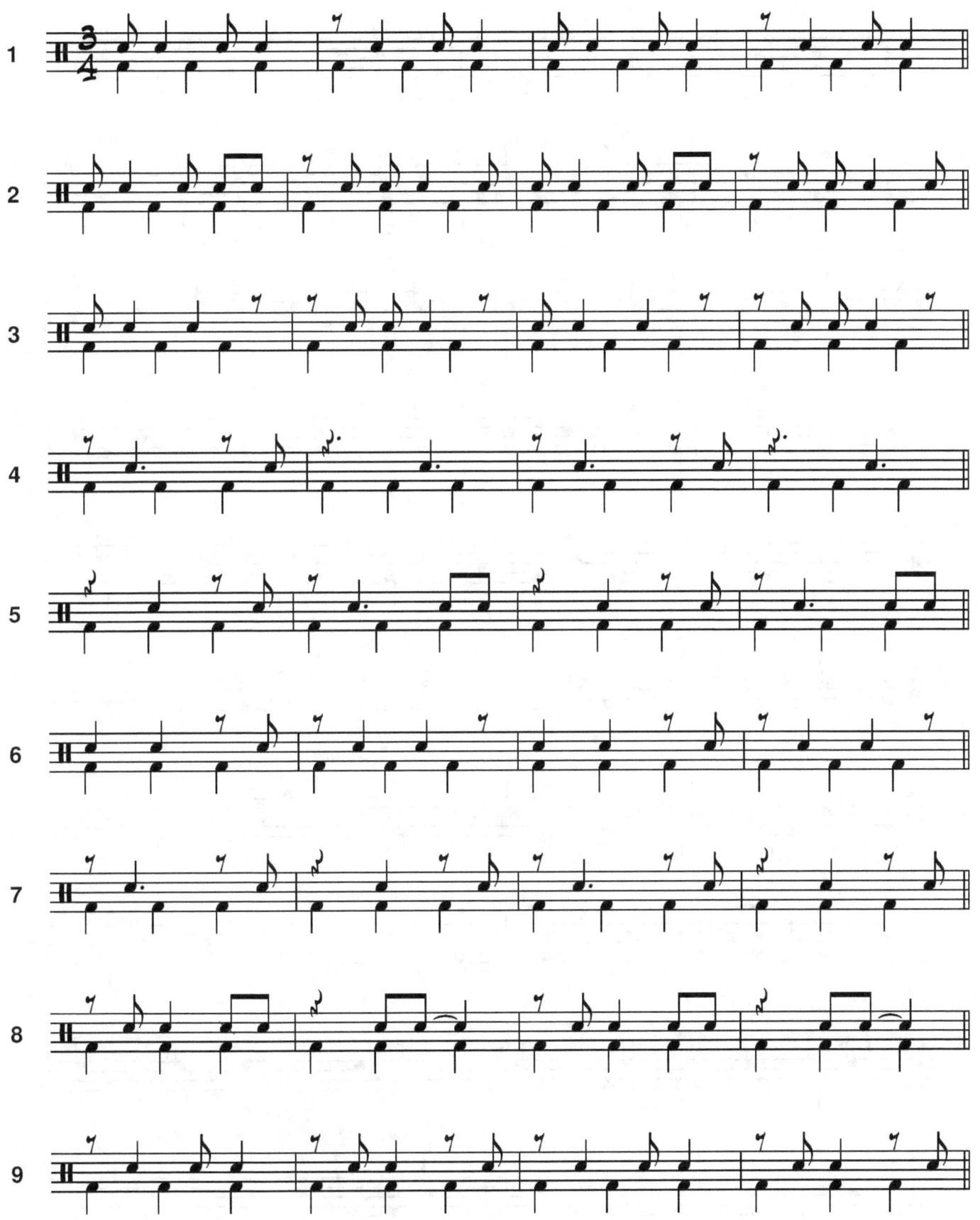

Syncopation Exercise 1

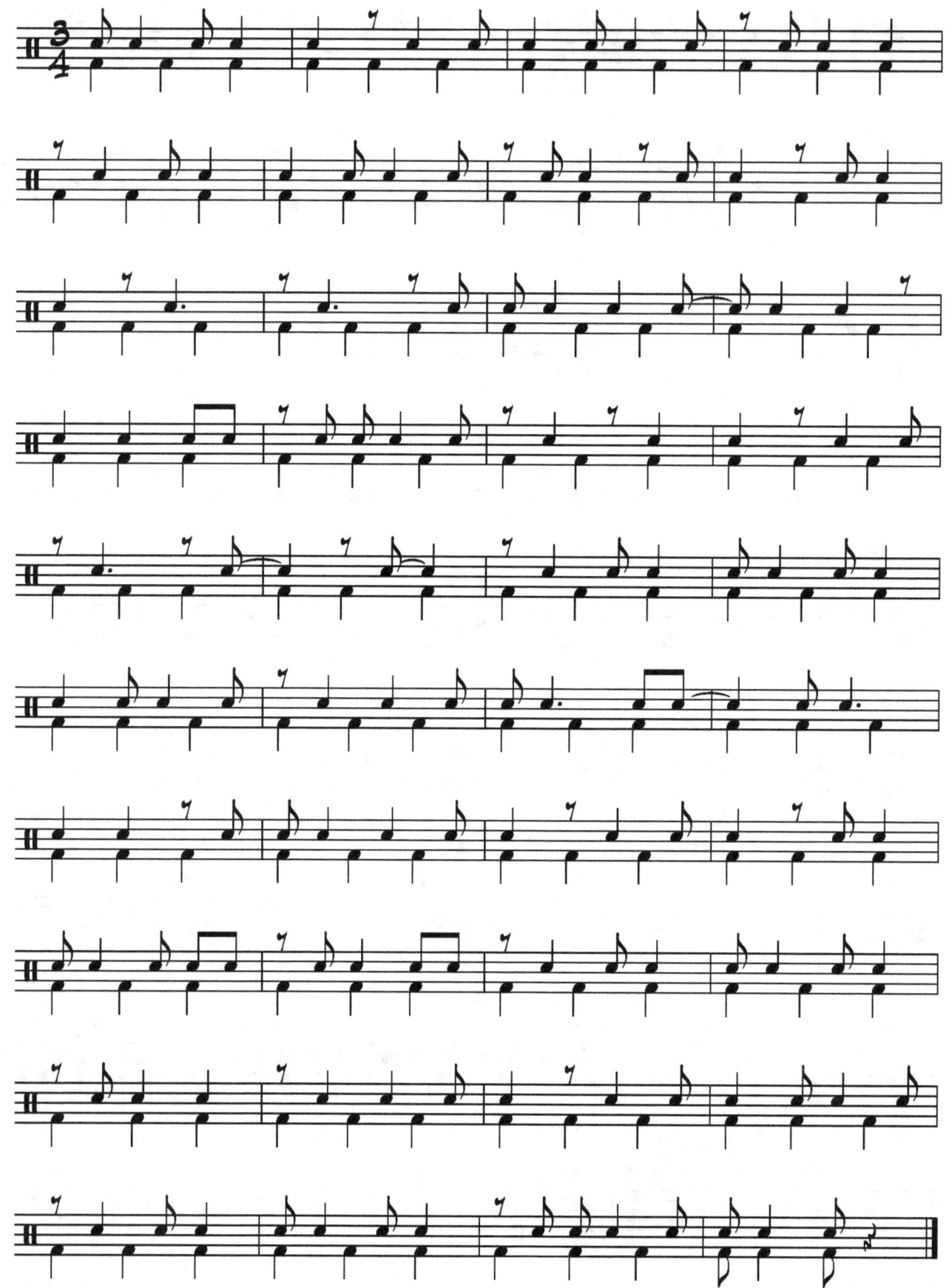

Syncopation Exercise 2

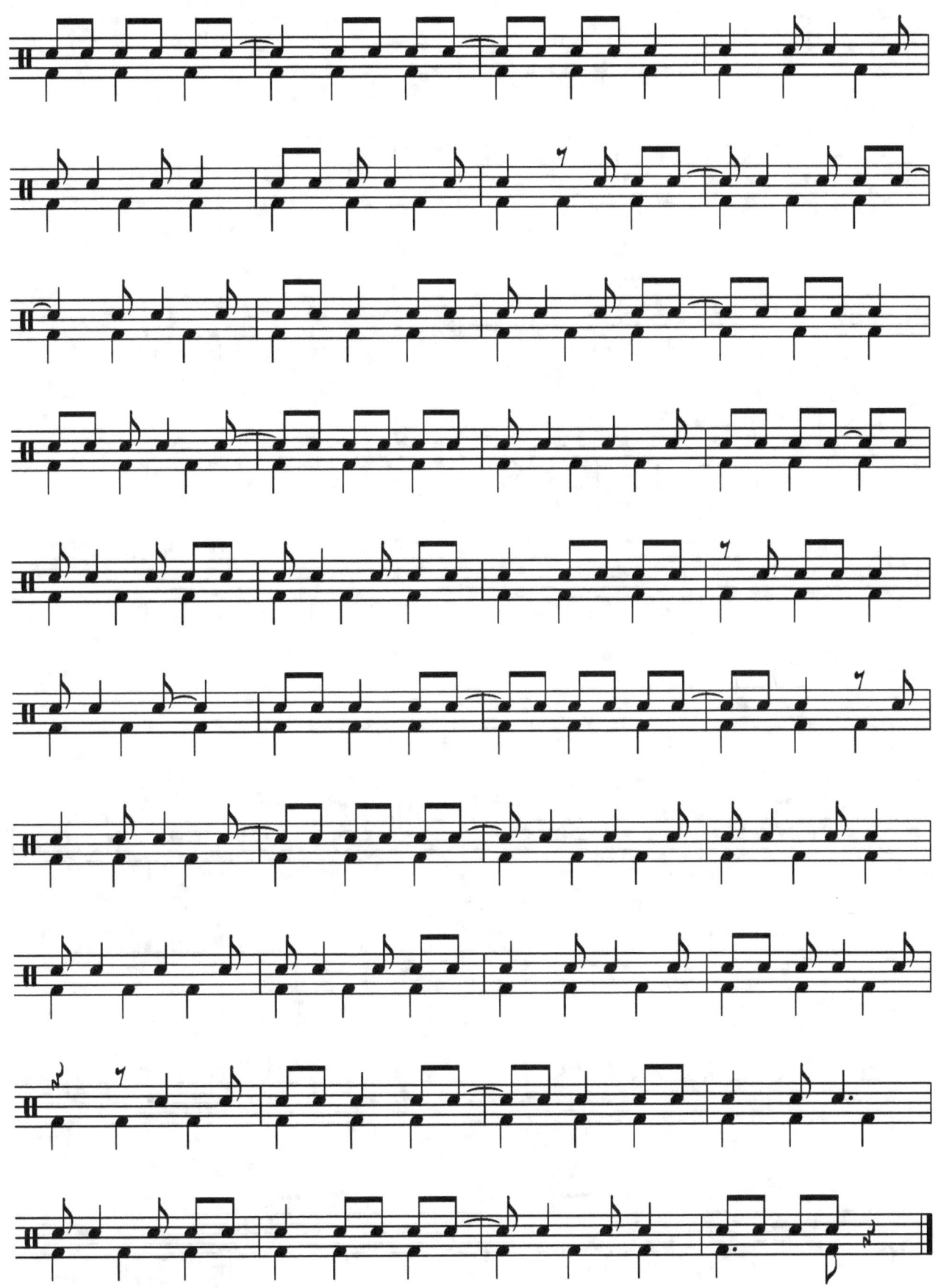

Syncopation Exercise 3

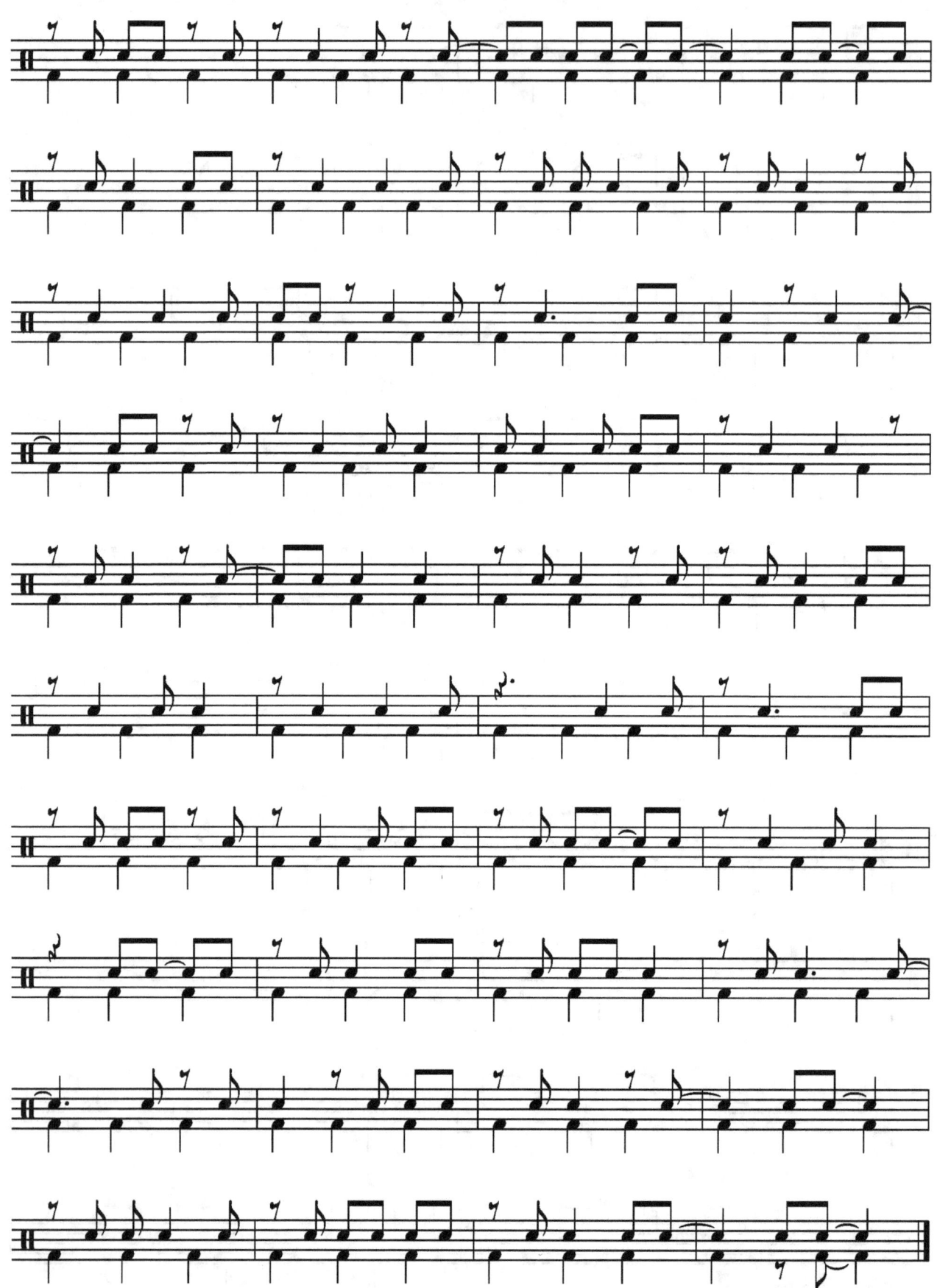

Syncopation Exercise 4

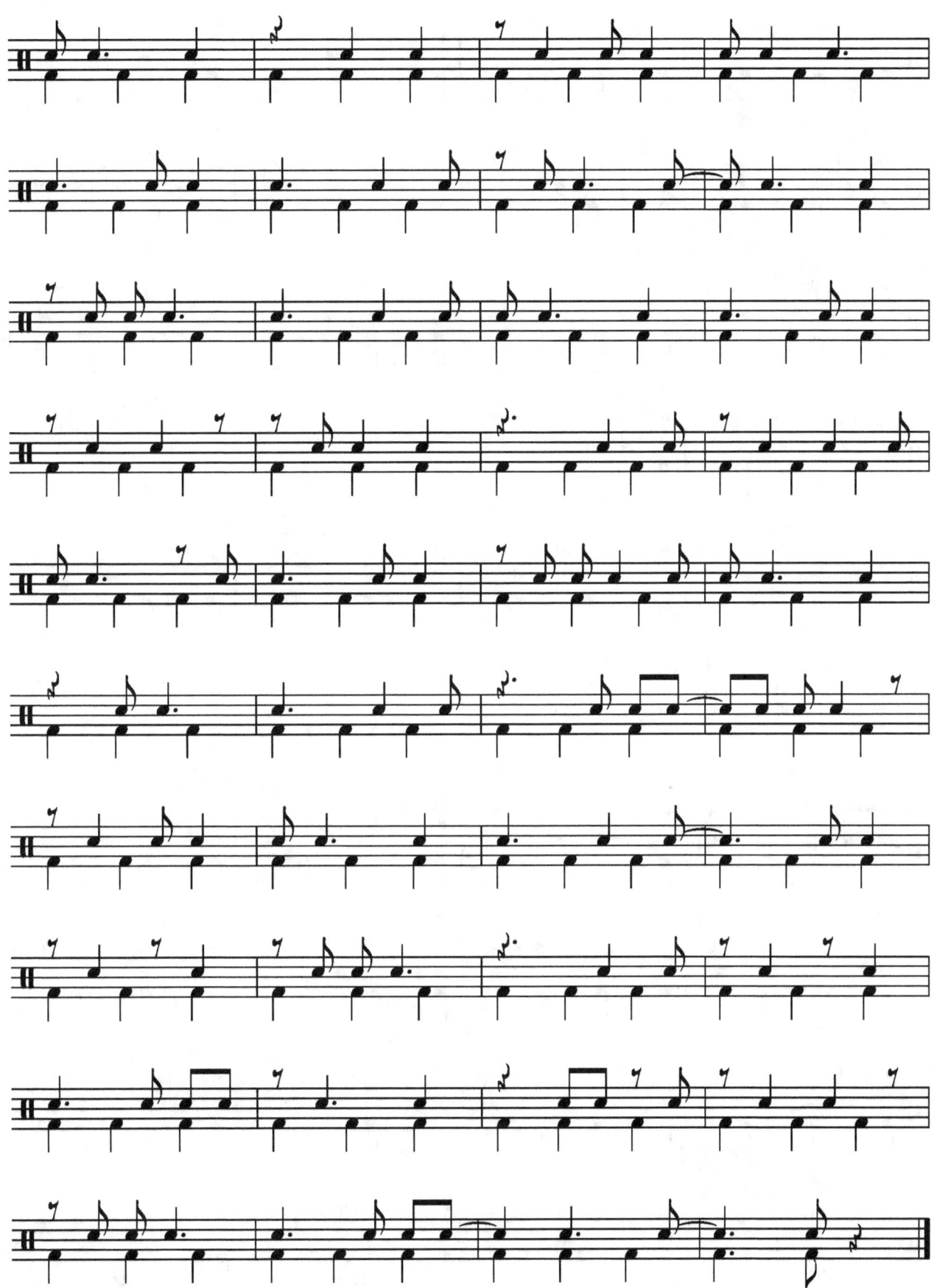

Syncopation Exercise 5

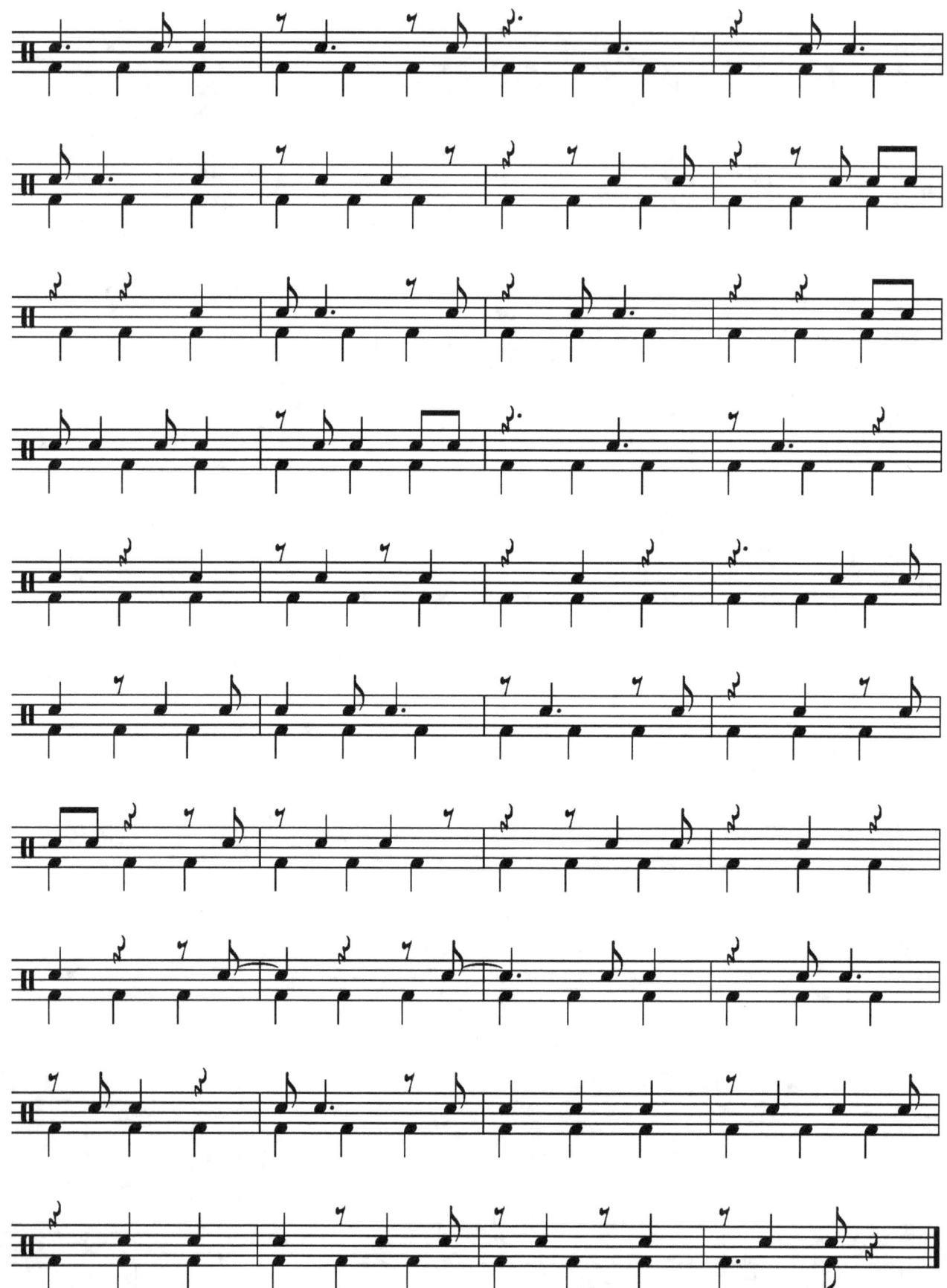

34

Syncopation Exercise 6

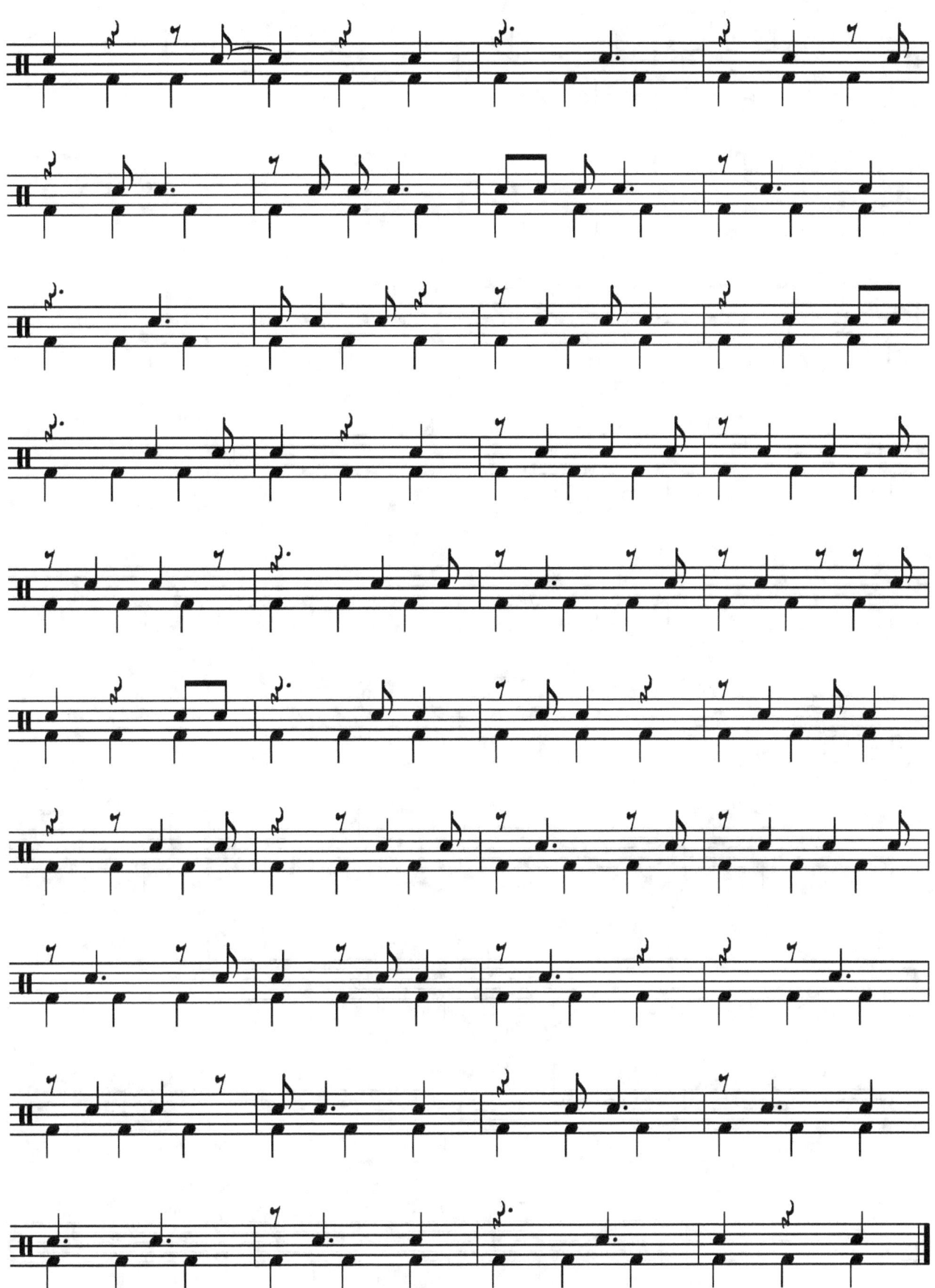

Syncopation Exercise 7

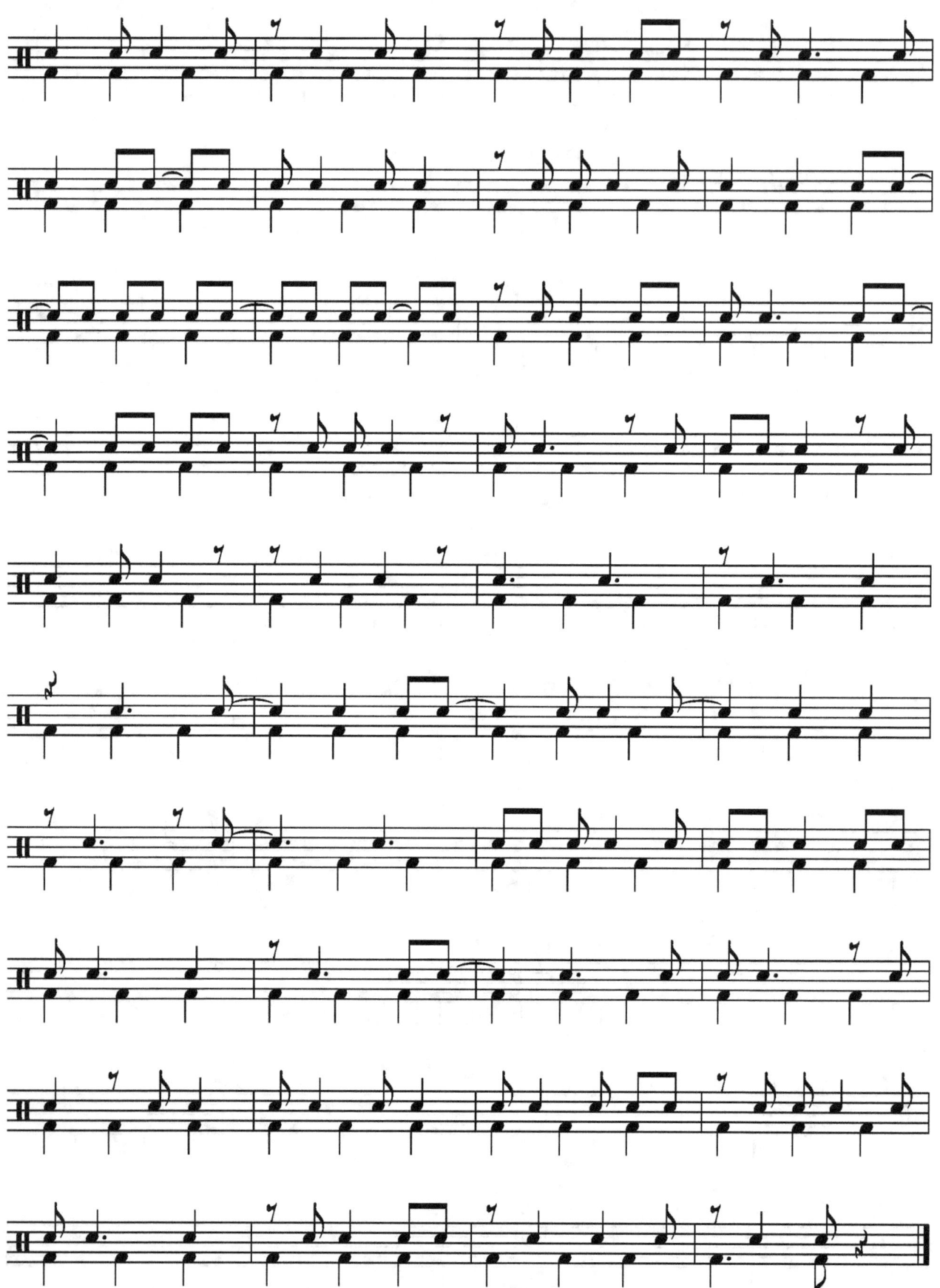

Syncopation Exercise 8

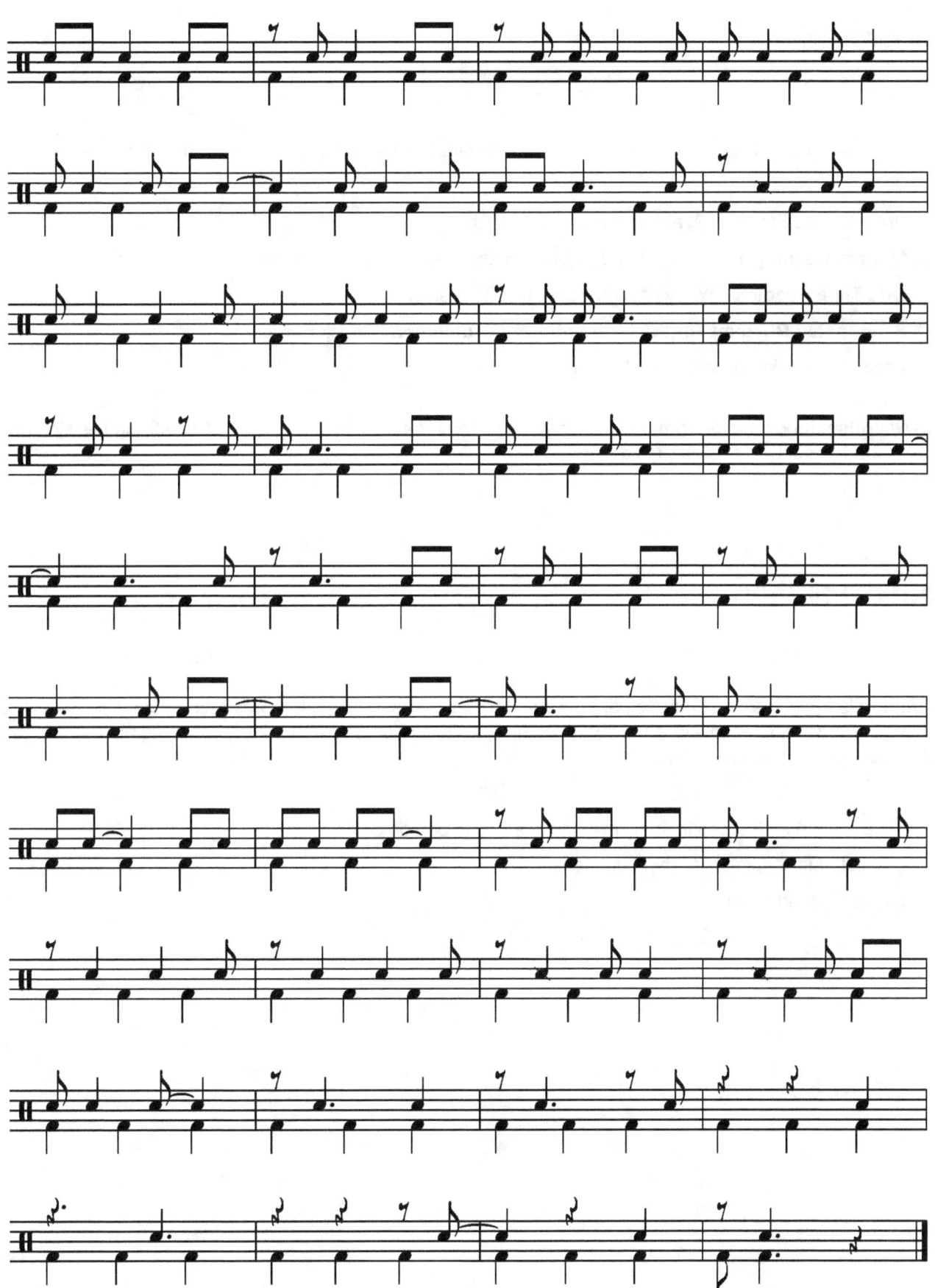

Bibliography

Excellent companions to this book, covering things not covered in this book, or differently than this book.

Progressive Steps to Syncopation by Ted Reed

Modern Reading Text in 4/4 by Louis Bellson and Gil Breines

Odd Time Reading Text by Louis Bellson and Gil Breines

Syncopated Rhythms for the Contemporary Drummer by Chuck Kerrigan

Creative Timekeeping by Rick Mattingly

Visit **www.cruiseshipdrummer.com** and search "Reed interpretations" for many ways of practicing this kind of materials, and for much more related to all areas of drumming.

About the author

Todd Bishop is a professional drummer, drum instructor, band leader, Origin Records recording artist, and visual artist living in Portland, Oregon. He is the author of the popular Cruise Ship Drummer! drumming blog, which you can visit at www.cruiseshipdrummer.com.

Contact Todd Bishop for lessons/instruction in this method in person or via Skype:

Email: toddbishop@cruiseshipdrummer.com

Skype ID: todd6ishop

Also visit: www.toddbishopjazz.com.